PEOPLE'S'HIT

"BASED ON THE TRUE AND HARSH REALITY OF SOCIETY"

UMANG JAIN

BLUEROSE PUBLISHERS
India | U.K.

Copyright © Umang Jain 2024

All rights reserved by author. No part of this publication may be reproduced, stored in a retrieval system or transmitted in any form or by any means, electronic, mechanical, photocopying, recording or otherwise, without the prior permission of the author. Although every precaution has been taken to verify the accuracy of the information contained herein, the publisher assumes no responsibility for any errors or omissions. No liability is assumed for damages that may result from the use of information contained within.

BlueRose Publishers takes no responsibility for any damages, losses, or liabilities that may arise from the use or misuse of the information, products, or services provided in this publication.

For permissions requests or inquiries regarding this publication,
please contact:

BLUEROSE PUBLISHERS
www.BlueRoseONE.com
info@bluerosepublishers.com
+91 8882 898 898
+4407342408967

ISBN: 978-93-6261-205-2

Cover design: Shivam
Typesetting: Namrata Saini

First Edition: July 2024

"Dedicated to My Family for Everything"

Always think all the possibilities...

[{DISCIPLINE >>> MOTIVATION???}]

PEOPLE'SHIT

[MINDSET>>>MONEY]

[HOPE>>>EXPECTATION]

"PEOPLE HAVE AN INCREDIBLE CAPACITY FOR GROWTH AND CHANGE. IT IS IN THEIR DEPTHS OF THEIR STRUGGLES AND CHALLENGES THAT They DISCOVER THEIR TRUE STRENGTH AND POTENTIAL"

About the Author

Umang Jain, a bright 16-year-old with thoughts well beyond his years, disrupts the self-help genre through his book called "Peopleshit". Jain plunges into the "true nature of the world," giving out valuable insights in "Peoples hit": However, be warned: coming  from his youth as well as scathing remarks on education systems ("It's a factory for slaves") may set off sparks. But then again, this is what makes him interesting! For teenagers yearning for new ideas and those who doubt conventional methods, these unorthodox opinions are like a breath of fresh air.

Think about how much impact we could have if we could polish that title up, soften the message a little bit and turn Jain loose on it. In this way he would unlock his true potential to achieve its desired aim; that being connecting with his target audience— young adults who are into self-help but need an alternative voice that goes against the grain. With a bit of editorial grace and some strategic marketing bombs dropped all over the place, Jain's unique perspective might just become the guiding star to generations .

7 PARTS

Introduction 1

PART – 1: You are Enough for Yourself 3

PART – 2: Does Mindset is a Real Shit? 19

PART – 3: Some Principle's for Living a Great and Happy Life 33

PART – 4: Start From Scratch 75

PART – 5: Diverse Personality 81

PART – 6: Does Love is a Scam?? 103

PART – 7: People's 'hit 119

The slave education system 149

Introduction

Welcome to the book peopleshit. I am *UMANG JAIN* your master/guide on this drastically transformative journey. The main aim of this book is to rebuild you all. Make sure you read the whole book through a few years of my own personal growth, exploration and countless triumphs over my own limitations. I have come to realize that mindset is everything. It is the foundation upon which we can live a life filled with happiness, fulfillment and success.

In a world bustling with endless possibilities, we find ourselves amidst a sea of voices, opinions and expectations. We often lose sight of our true essence, true taste, trapped in a cycle of self-doubt, overthinking and a perpetual longing for happiness. But what if I told you that you hold the power to break that shit and free yourself from this loop chains and rebuild yourself into the best version of which you are meant to be??

In this book we will delve into the depths of your psyche the pattern of overthinking that have held you back for far too long. Together we will discover the secrets to living a happy life not merely by chance, but by design. The path of happiness lies by cultivating a bold mindset that empowers you to conquer your fears, embrace your potential and master the art of living your life.

Prepare yourself for a journey that will push you beyond your comfort zone, challenge your beliefs and ignite a fire within you to reach new heights peopleshit is not only a book it is also a navigator or we can say A KEY to unlocking an extraordinary version within you it will teach how to fought with a real world not by Instagram life

Introduction

but a real life rewires your mind and develop the resilience needed to overcome and obstacles that stands in your way.

Becoming a master of your life requires a bunch of things but most importantly patience and discipline and the unwavering belief that you are capable of greatness so let's tap into the wellspring of your inner strength and change you into a powerful spirit that you were always meant to be.

So, Are you ready? To embrace your true potential? Are you prepared to let go of the past, break free from self-limitations and step into the life you were designed to live? If your answer is resounding "YES" then join me as we embark on this incredible journey together and if your answer is "NO" so scroll Instagram, watch fucking porn be the part of shit. Let peopleshit be your guiding light enlighten the path to life with Some genuine purpose joy and unyielding success.

From the author,

"UMANG JAIN"

"Your mindset is the lens through which you recognize the world it can either be a prison that limits your potential or a launching pad for extraordinary achievements choose it wisely for your mindset shapes your reality and determines the heights you can reach."
~~Umang Jain

PART - 1

You are Enough for Yourself

INTRODUCTION

Hello boys and girls! How are you all doing today? Not too great, I bet. Before we start this chapter, I want to ask you a simple question: how would you feel if you were a slave? Surprised by the question? Let me explain. Many of us are slaves to society and, more importantly, to our own minds. We often find ourselves trapped by expectations, fears, and doubts. People are unique creatures. We have the wisdom to achieve great things, but we also have the tendency to trick ourselves into thinking we are less than we are. Let's take a closer look at how this happens and explore ways to break free from these invisible chains. So, you all know that two scientists developed a theory stating that the fittest survive, or in simpler terms, the stronger ones make it through. But in today's world, physical strength is no longer the key player. The game is all about **money**. Let me explain why I mentioned the word "slave" and dive into the first stage of how we learn to be slaves. Okay, let's start, and we'll wrap it up in our "peopleshit" chapter.

The process begins the moment you step into school. Now, don't get me wrong—education itself isn't the villain here. It's the way education is dished out that's the problem. Our schools resemble prisons, much like the **Prussian Education System**. Nothing has changed since the 80s. We think that after school, we'll live our lives freely, but once we graduate, we realize we were just groomed to be slaves, not leaders. We'll delve deeper into this in the "peopleshit" phase.

In the 21st century, people bust their butts to become future slaves. Some sprinkle a bit of smart work into that hard work, only to end up working just as hard for their future slavery. Spot the difference? People are not hard to understand nor easy to decode. Today's generation is like a simple password that anyone can crack by entering "porn," "sex," and of course, "money." It's not my main point, but I find it absurd. Although I'm part of this "best" generation, I see people working hard without any real purpose, like they're traveling without knowing their destination. If you're well-prepared, you wouldn't need to slog away mindlessly.

Moreover, it's ridiculous how some people waste their time comparing and competing with each other. They're obsessed with being superior, while some poor souls end up traumatized from constant comparisons, leading them to dislike themselves. In this chapter, I'll give you the keys to embracing yourself and becoming better than before. Remember, "Nothing really completes you but yourself." So, without further ado, let's dive into our first phase: **You are enough for yourself**.

The Trap of Education

The Illusion of Freedom

From the moment we start school, we're fed the lie that education is our ticket to freedom. We believe that by the time we finish, we'll be equipped to live life on our terms. However, the reality is starkly different. The education system, modelled after the **Prussian system**, hasn't evolved. It's designed to produce obedient workers rather than innovative leaders. We spend years memorizing information and following rules, only to realize we've been conditioned to fit into a mould rather than encouraged to break it.

The Real Lesson

The real lesson we learn in school is how to conform. We're taught to sit still, follow orders, and not question authority. Creativity and critical thinking take a back seat to rote learning and standardized testing. This system doesn't prepare us for life; it prepares us to be cogs in a machine. By the time we graduate, we're so accustomed to following orders that we don't know how to lead our own lives.

The New Currency: Money

Physical Strength vs. Financial Power

In the past, survival depended on physical strength. Today, it's all about financial power. Money dictates everything—our education, healthcare, and even our happiness. The saying "money makes the world go round" has never been more accurate. We no longer need to be the strongest to survive; we need to be the wealthiest.

The Game of Wealth

This shift has turned life into a game of wealth accumulation. We chase after higher salaries, bigger houses, and more possessions, believing these will bring us happiness. But in the process, we become slaves to our jobs, working long hours and sacrificing our well-being for a pay check. We're caught in a cycle where money controls our lives, and we lose sight of what truly matters.

The Modern-Day Slave

Hard Work vs. Smart Work

In today's world, people pride themselves on their hard work. But what's the point of working hard if it only leads to more slavery? Some people mix in a bit of smart work, hoping it will free them from the grind. Yet, they still find themselves trapped, because they're working towards goals set by others rather than their own. The real trick is to work smart for your own dreams, not someone else's.

The Mind Game

People are not inherently difficult to understand, but they're not easy to unravel either. Modern society is like a simple password: easy to crack with the right keywords—sex, money, and power. These drives open up almost anyone's mind. It's almost laughable how predictable we've become. But the real joke is on us, as we work tirelessly without knowing our true destination. We're like travellers on an endless journey, unsure of where we're headed.

The Competition Trap

The Race to Nowhere

One of the biggest traps we fall into is the endless competition with others. We're taught to compare ourselves to everyone around us, striving to be better, richer, smarter. But this race is a dead end. Constantly measuring ourselves against others only breeds dissatisfaction and insecurity. Instead of finding our own path, we waste time and energy trying to outdo everyone else.

The Damage Done

This relentless comparison game isn't just exhausting; it's damaging. Some people, especially those who are more sensitive, suffer greatly from being constantly compared to others. They develop a deep-seated trauma and begin to dislike themselves, feeling they can never measure up. This cycle of comparison and self-doubt is toxic and needs to be broken.

Embracing Yourself

Finding Your Own Path

In this chapter, I'm going to give you the keys to breaking free from these chains. It's time to embrace yourself and your unique journey. Remember, "Nothing really completes you but yourself." Stop looking outside for validation and start recognizing your own worth. You are enough just as you are.

The Journey Begins

So, without further ado, let's dive into our first phase: **You are enough for yourself**. It's time to break free from the societal norms that bind us and start living life on our terms. Let's explore how we can reclaim our lives and become the leaders of our o

YOU ARE ENOUGH FOR YOURSELF

Comparison a word that is paradise for the perfect ones but the hell for the ones who are not perfect. The society, your parents, your friends and closed ones also draw a line of comparison. With those comparisons you feel that you are a shit and only a burden in this society and sometimes the person kills thyself but hold on why this happened no matter how tough you are at one certain point you felt that same shit but have you thought why this happens it does not happen spontaneously it begins with some parts or we can understand it with.

You are Enough for Yourself

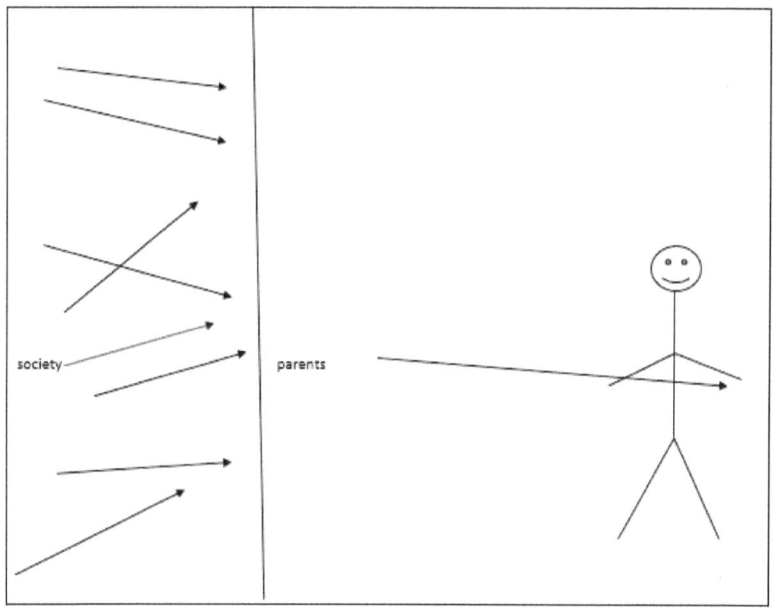

the figure I call this **figure the deadliest arrow** I think you easily understand this figure if you not .let me explain you that society loves to draw comparisons they give us some poisonous arrows like the arrow of self- doubt' the arrow of feel worthless, the arrow of anxiety, the arrow of sadness and etc. but your parents form a barricade to protect it to you and that's why you don't feel anything but after the arrows of society but your parents to throw a one deadliest arrow which is known as the arrow of not to trust which is enough to 1000 arrows of society .that one arrow of untrust can change a whole of the person and slowly- slowly that person is overwhelmed with many things which are not important to them like does am I able to do anything or not? I think I might die that really me! I am a loser!! Worries about future it happened because of the arrow of untrust later then you step a very harshful step that can ruin your whole life. So, never leave a trust on your child you really don't know who s/he really is and what s/he is really capable to do.

You are Enough for Yourself

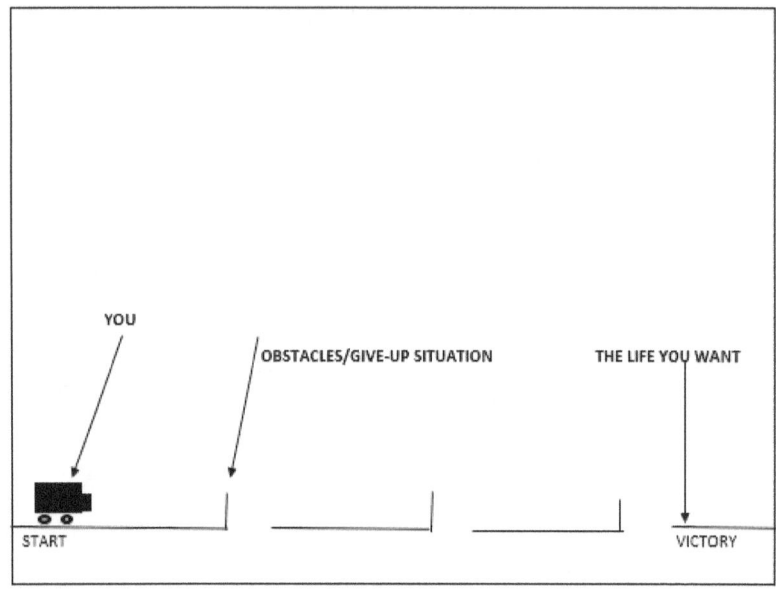

FIG 1.1

I call this figure [**A LUBRICANT CAR**] where car depicts you and the obstacles depicts any bad or worst situation in your life here a plane line depicts the person moving with full discipline to seek their victory and the vertical line depicts the momemt where the person loses their discipline here motivation help means sometimes making your discipline more longer you need a push and that push is motivation without motivation you can't do a work with discipline longer so basically lubricant car states that motivation is a bridge of discipline.whch make you disciplined for a longer run.

So, I hope you understand that being disciplined in a longer run you need a bridge of motivation . so when you need yourself better in a longer run so use a lubricant car. Okay so comparing yourself to others is like you forced yourself to do a thing that you can't really do .like once Einstein said "Don't push a fish to climb a tree while don't force a monkey to swin in water". Comparing yourself is like demeaning yourself since you have no clue what you can achieve . Typically in india , comparing their child is normal and I do agree that a healthy competition is good but sometimes it transform in a very harazduos way like everytime comparing their child in every activity not support him/her that leads in a negative way . It doesn't matter how poorly you perform in acaedemics it doesn't mean that you can't do anything if you want to find your true potential you need to connect with yourself maybe it helps you to find your real destiny and if you able to find your true potential so then keep going for it . And always remember toughest decisions of your life mostly came when you are broken or not in a good shape of your life so be tough buddy. The most important thing you need to be excellent at is **'HUMANITY'** yes simple word but no one in today's generation understand humans go too far to earn money and fame that they forget their humanity a real precious gemstone that only humans have . This is because keeping a spark of humanity is neccesary for maintaining society's civlty. It's important to keep in mind that you are enough just as you are in a culture that frequently emphasizes the need for externa validation and ongoing comparison . Embracing your boldness is a potent method to know your value since true confidence and self-assurance come from inside and if you are really a low confidence man/women you are getting distracted easily but always stay on your point you know the first step of your success starts when people starts to critise you or make joke of you just let them go let them you make them slaves .huh? don't ever try to doubt on yourself just **DOUBT** on yourself. I am going to share some vital points that will surely help you :

- ❖ Embracing individuality.
- ❖ Challenging self doubt .
- ❖ Embracing failure as growth.
- ❖ Don't make people as their god.
- ❖ People=balloons.

❖ Conclusion.

EMBRACING INDIVIDUALITY

Each of us are born with their uniqueness there is some uniqueness in every person. but in today's era people went too far to impress other people they just don't even love thyself they always spent their life to impress others thinking about others that what others should be thinking about them.

Life is a symphony, and each of us plays a unique instrument. Our individuality is the melody that we bring to the world's orchestra. It's the **solo performance** that only we can give, a tune composed of our choices, experiences, and dreams.

But how do we make this melody heard? How do we ensure it resonates?

1. **Celebrate Your Story**: Every chapter of your life, every triumph, and every stumble, is a note in your song. Celebrate it. Share your story with pride, and let others find rhythm in your resilience.

2. **Dance to Your Own Beat**: Don't just walk through life—dance! Move to the rhythm of your passions and let your steps be as unique as your fingerprint. Whether it's a tango or a tap, it's yours.

3. **Mix Your Palette**: Life is a canvas, and you're the artist. Mix the colors of your experiences to create a vibrant masterpiece. Don't shy away from bold hues; they make your painting stand out.

4. **Harmonize**: While your tune is unique, it's part of a larger chorus. Find harmony with others, blending your melodies to create something beautiful together.

5. **Compose Your Future**: Your individuality is not just about today; it's about the legacy you create. What will be the chorus of your life's symphony? Compose it with intention and joy.

Remember, individuality isn't just about standing apart; it's about standing tall, proud of the unique blend of qualities that make you, you. It's about adding your voice to the chorus of humanity and making the symphony of life richer for it.

So, what's the next note in your melody? How will you make your individuality sing today?

"In a world of copycats, dare to be the original masterpiece."

CHALLENGING SELF-DOUBT

Let's step out of the mythical realm and into the everyday hustle. Self-doubt isn't a dragon; it's that tiny pebble in your shoe—the one that irritates with every step. But fret not; we'll lace up our boots and tackle it head-on.

1. **The Job Interview Jitters:**
    - Imagine you're sitting across from the interviewer. Your heart races, palms sweat. Self-doubt whispers, *"They won't like you. You're not qualified."* But wait! Remember that time you aced a project? That's your armour. Speak confidently. You're not just answering questions; you're showcasing your superpowers.

2. **The Blank Canvas Syndrome:**
    - You're an artist, staring at that intimidating blank canvas. Doubt creeps in: *"What if it's terrible? What if no one gets it?"* But remember Van Gogh? His first strokes weren't masterpieces. He painted anyway. So, pick up that brush.

Each stroke is progress. Imperfect? Sure. But it's yours. Accept it and move forward

3. **The Social Gathering Anxiety**:
   - The party's buzzing, and you're in the corner, wondering if you belong. Self-doubt whispers, *"They're all smarter, funnier."* But guess what? Everyone's too busy worrying about their own dance moves. So, step onto the floor. Your rhythm matters. You might just start a conga line. Try to be your own king not anyone owns you!

4. **The Entrepreneurial Leap:**
   - You dream of starting a business. Doubt taps your shoulder: *"What if you fail? What if it flops?"* But think of Colonel Sanders. He was 65 when he launched KFC. Sixty-five! So, fry that chicken, my friend. Your secret blend of herbs and courage will season success.

Don't let ever self-doubt controls you be tough to handle it.

EMBRACING FAILURE AS A GROWTH

Failure is often seen as the end of the road, but what if I told you, it's actually a secret passageway to growth? Think of it as the ultimate teacher, handing out tough love lessons that shape us into wiser, stronger versions of ourselves.

Here's how to turn failure into a growth powerhouse:

1. **Fail Forward**: Every stumble is a step forward. Didn't get that job? It's a chance to refine your interview skills. Lost a game? It's an opportunity to come back stronger. Remember, **Thomas Edison** failed 1,000 times before the lightbulb moment!

2. **Reflect and Learn**: Post-failure is prime time for reflection. Ask yourself, "What worked? What didn't? Why?" This isn't about beating yourself up; it's about mining the experience for golden nuggets of wisdom.
3. **Resilience Gym**: Think of failure as a resilience workout. Every setback is a rep, making your 'never give up' muscle stronger. The more you lift, the tougher you get.
4. **Celebrate Effort**: Give yourself a pat on the back for trying. Effort is success in disguise. It's the courage to show up those counts.
5. **Plan B, C, D...**: If one path closes, scout for another. There's always another route to the summit. Be like water—adaptable, persistent, and always finding a way through.

Next time see failure as your dream killer but…. NOT YOUR AIM KILLER.

DON'T MAKE PEOPLE AS THEIR GODS

People are a very peculiar being in today's era people believe in two gods one who is real immortal god and one who are mortal. people are too lost in this era they lost their whole identity, power and their existence whoever they find good so called cool they simply make God It's simple: everyone's human, just like you. When we treat someone like they're perfect, like a god, we forget they can make mistakes too. It's not fair to them or to us. We all have our good points and our flaws, and that's okay. Remember, nobody's perfect, and that's what makes us all special in our own way. So, let's appreciate people for who they are, not as gods, but as fellow humans on this journey of life.

PEOPLE= BALLOONS

People are fragile, like balloons. Emotions can be easily pricked by sharp words or actions. Protect your emotional well-being and handle others with care. People are so fragile [I am too] they are very weak one small needle can be a reason for death of a person but we are not talking about real needle nor real physical death we are talking about the needle of emotions which be a reason for death of human emotions I can make it easy by using figures

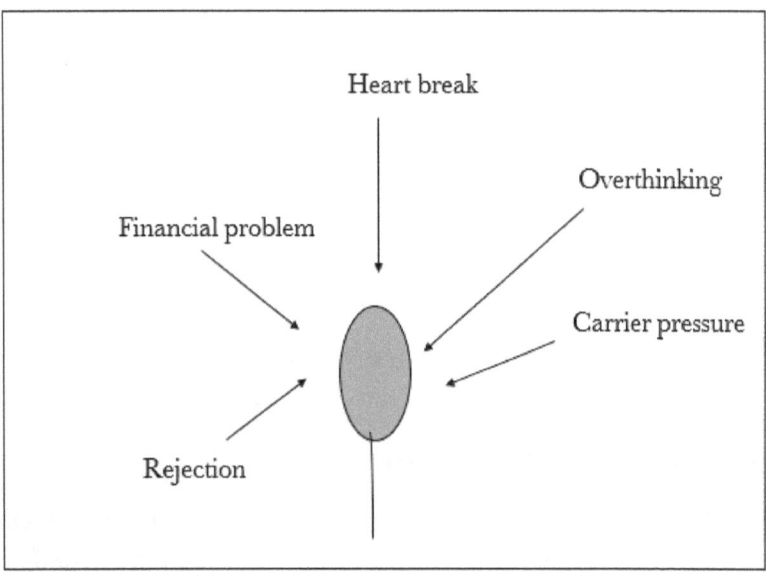

These are some very painful needles that can be a reason of death of their emotions.

CONCLUSION

In the journey of life, we often seek external validation and approval. Yet, hidden within us lies an unshakable truth: we are complete, just as we are. The essence of our being transcends societal expectations, achievements, and comparisons. In conclusion, the journey of self-discovery and self-improvement is a deeply personal one. It's about embracing your individuality, challenging self-doubt, and seeing failure as an opportunity for

growth. It's about not allowing society or others to define your worth or dictate your path.

Remember, you are not a slave to societal expectations or your own insecurities. You are the driver of your own life, and you have the power to steer it in the direction you choose.

In this journey, it's important to remember that you are enough just as you are. Your value doesn't decrease based on someone's inability to see your worth. So, dance to your own beat, paint your life with bold colours, and harmonize with those who resonate with your melody.

And most importantly, hold onto your humanity. In a world that often prioritizes material wealth and status, don't lose sight of the values that truly matter. Kindness, empathy, and love are the true measures of success.

So, go forth and embrace your journey with confidence and courage. Remember, the first step of your success starts when people start to criticize you or make a joke of you. Use it as a stepping stone to rise higher. You are enough for yourself, and you have the potential to achieve great things.

As you navigate through life, remember this: "The only person you should try to be better than is the person you were yesterday."

As the great Maya Angelou once said, "You alone are enough. You have nothing to prove to anybody." Remember this as you navigate through life. You are enough, just as you are. Amidst life's chaos, remember that your worth isn't determined by external measures. It resides in your authenticity, resilience, and capacity for self-love. Embrace imperfections—they are the brushstrokes that create your unique masterpiece.

"Within your soul's sanctuary, you hold the universe. Your scars, dreams, and laughter weave a tapestry of strength. You need no validation; your existence is validation enough. So, stand tall, honour your journey, and whisper to your heart: 'I am complete —I am enough.'" ~~Umang Jain

PART - 2

Does Mindset is a Real Shit?

Imagine your mind as a powerful director in the grand theatre of life. It's the one pulling the strings behind the scenes, shaping your experiences and influencing your choices. But what exactly is this elusive thing we call "mindset"?

In this chapter, we'll explore mindset—the lens through which we view the world. Is it just a trendy buzzword, or does it hold real power?

So firstly, understand what mindset is we start from scratch:

1. What is mind?
2. What is mindset.
3. Does mindset is a real shit??
4. Rich mindset vs poor mindset!!
5. Conclusion

So, we start from a word "MIND" which is the piolet of our brains plays like an instrument. The mind is an intricate entity that orchestrates cognitive functions and emotional responses, shaping human experience. Key aspects include:

1. **Perception**: It processes sensory data to form a coherent picture of the external world. Basically, it is the retina of your brain
2. **Emotions**: It regulates feelings, influencing behaviour and decision-making. The part where most people lose their control.
3. **Memory**: It stores and retrieves information, forming the basis of learning and knowledge. An SSD
4. **Desires and Intentions**: It drives motivations, guiding goal-oriented behaviour.
5. **Reasoning and Choices**: It employs logic and creativity to solve problems and make decisions.

6. **The Unconscious**: It operates below the level of conscious awareness, affecting actions and thoughts.

The mind's functions are critical in navigating the complexities of life, enabling individuals to interact with their environment and society effectively.

That could be the best illustrative in relative to mind.

Now we move after what is mindset??

Mindset is a very powerful thing that can make you a king or convert into a beggar mindset is not only set of beliefs but also a set of perceptions which come forward according to your mindset but they're still a question what is really mind-set is?

In simple words mindset shapes every aspect of your life, from how you tackle challenges to how you interact with others or we can also say that mind act like law-maker and mindset follows it. It's not just about positive thinking; it's about setting the stage for how you live your life and achieve your goals. Mindset is everything cause basically it is our third eye the most powerful eye. In this era most people limit their mind because they contain fixed mindset not growth mindset, but what are they? What is growth mindset? What is fixed mindset?

According to Carol s. Dweck, there are two basic mindsets: fixed and growth. If you have a fixed mindset, you believe your abilities are fixed traits and therefore can't be changed. You may also believe that your talent and intelligence alone lead to success, and effort is not required.

On the flip side, if you have growth mindset, you believe that your talents and abilities can be developed over time through effort and persistence. People with this mindset don't necessarily believe that everyone can become Einstein or Mozart just because they try. They do, however, believe that everyone can get smarter or more talented if they work at it.

I'll tell you the story of Alden and Elara's that can make everything easy related to fixed and growth mindset:

In a small town nestled between rolling hills and whispering woods, there lived a clockmaker named Alden. Alden was known far and wide for his exquisite timepieces, each one more intricate than the last. But despite his skill, Alden harboured a secret that weighed heavily on his heart—he believed that his abilities were limited, that his talent had reached its peak, and that he could never surpass the mastery of his grandfather, the legendary clockmaker who founded their family shop.

Alden's fixed mindset kept him from experimenting with new designs or techniques. He followed the same patterns and methods that had been passed down through generations, fearing that any deviation might lead to failure. The townspeople, who once marvelled at the clockmaker's creations, began to notice that the spark of innovation was missing from his work.

One day, a curious and spirited young apprentice named Elara came to work with Alden. Elara was full of ideas and had an infectious enthusiasm for learning. She saw potential in every gear and spring, and her imagination knew no bounds. Unlike Alden, Elara believed that with effort and perseverance, she could learn anything and improve her skills endlessly.

Elara's growth mindset began to influence the atmosphere of the shop. She encouraged Alden to take risks and to see mistakes not as failures but as opportunities to grow. "What if," she would often say, "we are only confined by the walls we build ourselves?"

As the seasons changed, so did Alden's outlook. Inspired by Elara's perspective, he slowly started to challenge his old beliefs. He experimented with new materials, embraced complex mechanisms, and even began to teach others the art of clockmaking, something he had never considered before.

The transformation was not immediate, and Alden faced many setbacks along the way. But with each challenge, he felt his skills sharpening, his creativity expanding, and his world growing a little bit larger. The town once again buzzed with excitement, eager to see what marvellous creation Alden would unveil next.

In time, Alden became known not only as a master clockmaker but also as a mentor who inspired others to believe in their limitless potential. And as for Elara, she continued to spread her growth mindset, reminding everyone that the true measure of success is not in the ticking of a clock but in the journey of continual learning and self-improvement.

And so, the story of Alden and Elara teaches us that our mindset shapes our destiny. While a fixed mindset can keep us trapped in the comfort of the familiar, a growth mindset opens the door to a world of endless possibilities.

Let's again recap what is fixed mindset and growth mindset cause when you truly understand you also gain wisdom to change it.

Here are some fixed vs. growth mindset examples.

Fixed Mindset	Growth Mindset
Either I'm good at it or I'm not.	I can learn to do anything I want.
That's just who I am. I can't change it.	I'm a constantly evolving work in progress.

If you have to work hard, you don't have the ability.	The more you challenge yourself, the smarter you become.
If I don't try, then I won't fail.	I only fail when I stop trying.
That job position is totally out of my league.	That job position looks challenging. Let me apply for it.

The problem in this generation is most of them are fixed mindset persons their mind does not support growth mindset. Growth mindset is useful in all directions in business, in a relationship, in personal life and in professional life so how to fix it?? And most of the people said I am a growth mindset man/woman but actually they are not so here I create a big type of sequence in which the journey start FIXED ➔ GROWTH MINDSET.

Chapter 1: The Locked Vault

Imagine a dusty old vault in your mind. It's labelled "Fixed Mindset." The door creaks, and inside, Grumble beard—the resident critic—sits grumbling. His favourite hobby? Telling you why you can't do things. But guess what? You're about to change the locks.

Signs You're in the Fixed Zone

1. **Grumble beard's Whispers**: Ever hear that voice saying, "You're terrible at this"? Yep, that's Grumble beard. He's like a grumpy theatre critic who hates one-person shows.

2. **Avoidance Alley**: You tiptoe around challenges, avoiding the spotlight of failure. It's like hiding from a cosmic pop quiz.

Chapter 2: The Growth Mindset Map

1. **Positive Potion Brew:**
   - Mix optimism, curiosity, and stardust.
   - Sip it daily. Believe challenges are cosmic invitations to level up.
2. **Analysis Transformation:**
   - Turn grumble beard's critiques into gold.
   - When he says, "You're terrible," reply, "Ah, my next adventure awaits!"
3. **Mistake Magic:**
   - Transform mistakes into spellbinding lessons.
   - Each blunder is a plot twist—a chance to rewrite your story.

Chapter 3: The Quest for Growth

1. **The Bridge of Positivity:**
   - Cross it. Look for rainbows after storms.
   - Even when life hands you lemons, make cosmic lemonade.
2. **The Forest of Effort:**
   - Here, trees whisper ancient wisdom: "Effort is the stick that turns acorns into oaks."
   - Plant seeds, water them, and watch resilience bloom.
3. **The Cave of Curiosity:**
   - Enter. Explore. Unearth hidden talents.
   - grumble beard grumbles, but you're too busy spelunking.

Epilogue: The Growth Mindset Medicine

1. **Brew It Daily**:
   - Mix gratitude, courage, and stardust.
   - Feel your neurons high-five each other.
2. **Dance with Uncertainty**:
   - Vibe with challenges. They're your cosmic dance partners, leading you to undiscovered constellations.

Your Quest Awaits

Unlock the vault. Toss grumble beard a feathered hat (he'll look dashing). Embrace growth. The universe applauds your encore.

Remember, dear reader, you're not stuck—your stardust in motion.

After it we reach the question that does mindset is a real shit??

As we collect the lots of information about mind and mindset so now you decide does mindset is a real shit or not for me it helps me to hit but who knows for someone it is a piece of shit.

Rich mindset vs poor mindset

The distinction between a rich mindset and a poor mindset primarily lies in attitudes, beliefs, and behaviour's regarding money, success, and personal growth. Here are some key differences:

Attitudes Toward Money:

Rich Mindset:

- Views money as a tool for creating opportunities and achieving goals.

- Believes in the potential for wealth creation through investments and entrepreneurship.
- Focuses on growing wealth and generating passive income.

Poor Mindset:

- Sees money primarily as a means to cover immediate needs and wants.
- Often views wealth as something beyond reach or believes it is only attainable through luck.
- Focuses on earning and spending, with little emphasis on saving or investing.

Approach to Learning and Growth:

Rich Mindset:

- Emphasizes continuous learning and self-improvement.
- Seeks out new knowledge, skills, and experiences to enhance personal and professional development.
- Values education and is open to feedback and constructive criticism.

Poor Mindset:

- May be resistant to change and new ideas.
- Relies on existing knowledge and skills, with little effort to learn or grow.
- May view education and self-improvement as unnecessary or unattainable.

Risk and Opportunity:

Rich Mindset:

- Willing to take calculated risks to achieve greater rewards.
- Sees failures and setbacks as learning opportunities and stepping stones to success.
- Actively looks for opportunities and is proactive in seizing them.

Poor Mindset:

- Tends to avoid risks, preferring safety and security even if it means limited growth.
- Views failures as permanent setbacks and may be discouraged easily.
- Often waits for opportunities to come rather than seeking them out.

Time Perspective:

Rich Mindset:

- Thinks long-term, planning for future goals and financial independence.
- Practices delayed gratification, investing time and resources now for future benefits.
- Focuses on building sustainable wealth and legacy.

Poor Mindset:

- Focuses on short-term needs and desires, often at the expense of long-term goals.

- Prefers immediate gratification, spending money and time on instant rewards.
- May lack a clear plan for future financial stability or growth.

Relationships and Networking:

Rich Mindset:

- Values building and nurturing a strong network of relationships.
- Understands the importance of collaboration and mutual support in achieving success.
- Sees others as potential partners, mentors, or sources of inspiration.

Poor Mindset:

- May have a more isolated or competitive view of relationships.
- May see others as competition or threats rather than potential allies.
- Less likely to invest time and effort in building a supportive network.

Mindset on Challenges and Problems:

Rich Mindset:

- Views challenges as opportunities to innovate and grow.
- Maintains a positive attitude, believing in their ability to overcome obstacles.
- Focuses on solutions and possibilities rather than problems.

Poor Mindset:

- Sees challenges as insurmountable problems or excuses for inaction.
- May have a more negative outlook, doubting their ability to succeed.
- Focuses on the difficulties and obstacles rather than potential solutions.

Taste:

Rich mindset:

- rich mindset offers you a very different and valued things. Rich mindset never does a show off thing those who are top riches who never show off they live a life of Quiet luxury "always remember rich mindset never makes a noise it makes a sound"

Poor mindset:

- poor mindset also offers you a very different useless thing. poor mindset is obsessed with show off things they want to show how much money they got they want to look like rich but they can't "always remember poor mindset always makes a lot of noise"

These differences highlight how a rich mindset can lead to behaviours and choices that promote financial success and personal fulfilment, while a poor mindset may result in limitations and missed opportunities.

CONCLUSION

Mindset is your very precious and powerful tool that can make you or destroy you try to be master in your mindset by doing meditation not doing masturbation do exercise cause scrolling insta/you- tube doesn't make the world work although. life is all about having fun in life but do not go too far for getting fun whether it leads pain in your ASS.

In the story of life's grand theatre, your mind is the director, and your mindset is the script. It's not just a fancy word; it's the power behind your every act. Here's a simple wrap-up of what we've learned:

1. **Mind**: It's like the pilot of your brain's airplane. It helps you see, feel, remember, want things, and make choices. It's super important for dealing with life's big puzzle.

2. **Mindset**: This is like your brain's pair of glasses. It changes how you see everything. It's not just about being positive; it's about how you set up your life and chase your dreams. It's like having a superpower eye that guides you.

3. **Fixed vs. Growth Mindset**: Some people think their smarts and skills are just what they're born with—like a fixed pie. That's a fixed mindset. But others believe they can grow their abilities over time, like levelling up in a game. That's a growth mindset.

4. **Changing Mindsets**: If you're stuck in a fixed mindset, like thinking you're not good at something, you can change it! Start by mixing up some optimism, looking at challenges as chances to grow, and turning mistakes into magic lessons.

5. **Rich mindset vs Poor mindset**: In summary, a rich mindset is characterized by long-term thinking, continuous learning, and a proactive approach to opportunities and challenges. It emphasizes financial discipline, investment, and building strong relationships. In contrast, a poor mindset focuses on short-term needs, resists change, avoids risks, and often views challenges negatively. These differences in attitudes, beliefs, and behaviours can significantly impact one's financial success and personal fulfilment, with a rich mindset leading to greater opportunities and growth, while a poor mindset may result in limitations and missed chances.

So, remember, whether you think you can grow and learn new things or not, you're right. It's all about the mindset you choose. And just like Alden, you can switch from a fixed mindset to a growth mindset and open up a whole new world of possibilities.

PART - 3

Some Principle's for Living a Great and Happy Life

Some Principle's for Living a Great and Happy Life

In this enchanting chapter, we'll explore timeless principles that weave magic into our existence. Imagine waking up each day with a secret smile, ready to embrace life's grand adventure. But first, let me ask you:

"What if happiness were a compass, guiding us toward greatness? How would you navigate your journey?" for my point of view the compass is within you. Let me elaborate it Imagine a world where joy isn't just a fleeting emotion but a North Star—a beacon that leads us to our best selves. Picture this: **Happiness as the celestial compass, pointing us toward greatness.**

Now, close your eyes and feel the magnetic pull. It whispers, *"Seek purpose, not perfection."* It nudges you to explore uncharted territories, to dance with vulnerability, and to embrace the symphony of your own existence.

Remember, my friend, the compass is within you. Let it guide you toward greatness, one constellation at a time.

"Happiness is not something ready-made. It comes from your own actions." — Dalai Lama

Hope you get it the answer of question or for your point of view it can be different

Let's move on our principles: -

1. Always keep mindset superior not money.
2. Interconnection b/w hope, perception, expectation.
3. Not always be gen-z.
4. Jain's law.
5. Spirituality never regrets you.
7. the white board syndrome.

8. don't be an NPC.

9. Heavy Rocket.

10. hit coin.

11. the castle of patience.

12. THE UMANG FORMULA.

13. Be like time.

14. Trust-meter.

15. Real gold mine.

16. The last option.

17. A clean life?

18. Anger acceleration.

MINDSET>>>MONEY

Mindset as we talk lot of it you've better understand that a rich mindset can make a poor to a rich but a poor mindset make a rich to poor always remember having lot of money don't every-time makes you rich in a longer run for that you need a mindset that is able to control it but in today's era people are not able to understand this cause they are busy in making reel's making streaks on snapchat this era loves to spend money but not theirs[cause they are unable to earn money] but their parent's and with their parents money they do fucking show-off their money how crazy it is huh? Always remember rich mindset always beliefs in a quiet luxury rich mindset never makes noise [the noise that today's generation make doing showing off their parental money] it makes sounds which are very pleasant to hear.

So, keep always your mind superior and come-out from this short giving pleasurable things [scrolling insta/you tube, watching porn, procrastinate, eating junk crap living fully in dead zone {comfortable zone}] and work for long-term giving pleasurable things [spend the time with your passion do the work for that think about your parents]

HOPE >EXPECTATION=PERCEPTION

Having hope towards someone or something is very full of peace but if you just replace a word hope to expectation it leads an endless way of pain with moving every step pain increases and increases *"Hope is like a whisper in the heart, while expectation is a loud demand. Hope allows room for miracles, while expectation often leads to disappointment."* Remember, hope keeps our spirits alive, even when circumstances seems challenging. Hope is a gentle flame that guides us forward, whereas expectation can sometimes weigh us down.

If you want to change your perception you need to change your expectation first. expectation is like big brother of perceptions how you expect that very leads only in a negative perception instead of that you can switch hope in place into expectation then the problem resolves itself

HOPE< = >PERCEPTION

GEN-Z IS SHIT OR THEY DO HIT??

Pros of Gen Z: Generation-z like it is the generation where everything is going on literally everything this and alpha generation are habitat to live in a comfortable zone like do whatever they want they are addicted to phone eating whatever they want there is no sign of discipline in them I am not saying all of this generation are shit but there are a few peoples are in this generation who are going to be a masterpiece I bet you this generation is the most powerful generation if they get back to their track and I don't think that they are going to get back on a track as I said this is the most powerful generation if they are on their true tracks if not so it can be proven for the crash of this society like everything has its two sides good and worst this generation is too bended in the worst side: here are some pros and cons of generation- z

PROS

1. Technologically Savvy: Gen Z grew up with the internet, smartphones, and social media. They are comfortable using technology and can easily adapt to new software and skills.
2. Diversity and Inclusion: Gen Z is the most diverse generation in history. Exposure to various cultures and backgrounds has made them more accepting and empathetic.
3. Entrepreneurial Spirit: Many Gen Z individuals are interested in starting their own businesses, leading to increased innovation and economic growth.
4. Socially Conscious: Gen Z is aware of social and environmental issues and takes action to address them

Cons of Gen Z:

1. Short Attention Span: Constant information influx from social media has led to shorter attention spans, making it challenging for them to focus on tasks for extended periods.
2. Lack of Real-Life Wisdom: Despite confidence, they lack practical life experience to handle challenges effectively.
3. Cyber Challenges: Gen Z faces cyberbullying, internet addiction, and privacy risks due to their heavy reliance on technology.
4. Show-off culture: - Generation Z tends to place a high value on showcasing their lifestyles, often through social media, which can inadvertently contribute to anxiety and depression among their peers. The pressure to appear

wealthy or successful can lead to feelings of inadequacy for those who perceive themselves as falling short. This constant comparison and the pursuit of validation can be mentally exhausting.

Moreover, many members of Generation Z are accustomed to the comforts of their established routines. When they are forced to step out of their comfort zones, it can lead to significant upheaval and stress in their lives. This transition often reveals both strengths and weaknesses, but the initial disruption can feel overwhelmingly negative.

Looking ahead, Generation Alpha, though still very young, is predicted to face even greater challenges. As they grow up in a world dominated by digital interaction and rapid technological advancement, the pressures and mental health concerns experienced by Generation Z may be amplified. There is a concern that the youngest generation will struggle even more with issues related to self-worth, social comparison, and emotional resilience.

JAIN'S LAW

Jain's Law Explained

Jain's Law posits that the trajectory of any new endeavour—whether a career, project, or personal goal—can be predicted based on the initial time investment. It emphasizes the relationship between the pace at which one begins their journey and the subsequent outcomes. The law can be summarized as follows:

Rapid Start, Short Journey: If you start a new endeavour quickly, moving from 0 to 1 in your journey with little time or effort, the subsequent journey from 1 to 100 will also be swift. However, this rapid progression often leads to an equally fast decline from 100 back to 0. In essence, quick initial success is usually unsustainable and can result in a short-lived peak followed by a rapid fall.

Slow Start, Long Journey: Conversely, if the initial phase from 0 to 1 is prolonged, involving significant time and effort, the progression from 1 to 100 will be more stable and enduring. The time spent reaching 100 is considerably longer, and the decline from 100 to 0 is either very slow or may never occur. This suggests that a slow, steady start builds a strong foundation, leading to sustained success and long-term stability.

Practical Implications of Jain's Law

1. Fast Success Risks: Achieving success too quickly can lead to burnout, a lack of sustainable practices, and an inability to cope with subsequent challenges. This often results in a quick collapse as the initial success was not built on a solid foundation.

2. Sustainable Growth: Taking the time to build a career or project slowly allows for learning, adaptation, and the establishment of strong practices. This patience can result in sustained success and long-term fulfilment.

Key Takeaways

-Fast Success: While it can bring immediate rewards and recognition, it is often precarious. The journey may end as quickly as it began, leading to disappointment and potential failure.

- Slow Success: This approach involves patience, resilience, and continuous effort. It builds a robust foundation, leading to enduring success and deeper satisfaction.

The Broader Perspective

Jain's Law underscores the importance of patience and perseverance. It suggests that individuals should be mindful of their approach to new endeavour's, recognizing that quick success can be fleeting and potentially harmful, while slow, deliberate progress is more likely to yield lasting and meaningful outcomes.

Personal Responsibility

"You are responsible for everything that is happening or will happen in your life."

This principle emphasizes personal accountability. Your choices, actions, and the pace at which you pursue your goals directly influence the outcomes. By embracing this responsibility, you can make more informed decisions about how to approach. Make a right decision for yourself remember no one is responsible for your happiness and sadness until you give them your key by which they can control you.

Conclusion

Jain's Law provides a valuable framework for understanding the dynamics of success and failure. It encourages a measured and patient approach to new ventures, highlighting the benefits of sustainable growth over rapid, short-lived achievements. By applying this law, individuals can cultivate long-term success and avoid the pitfalls of fleeting triumphs.

Spirituality never regrets you

Spirituality, unlike many other paths in life, carries no regrets. It's the gentle whisper within us, urging us towards understanding and acceptance, rather than dwelling on what could have been.

Spirituality transcends religious doctrines and esoteric rituals; it's a universal journey of self-discovery and a connection to something greater than ourselves.

At its core, spirituality invites us to explore the depths of our own being, to confront our fears, and to embrace our vulnerabilities. It teaches us to let go of the burdens of the past and the anxieties of the future, anchoring us firmly in the present moment. This mindful presence allows us to experience life more fully and authentically.

Through practices as simple as mindfulness, meditation, or acts of kindness, spirituality offers a refuge from the chaos of everyday life, guiding us towards inner peace and stability. It doesn't require elaborate ceremonies or complex philosophies; rather, it thrives on simplicity and sincerity. By aligning our thoughts, actions, and intentions with our deepest values and aspirations, spirituality becomes a compass, guiding us through life's inevitable storms with grace and resilience.

Spirituality is a journey open to all, regardless of background or belief. It invites us to explore the vastness of our own existence and discover the profound interconnectedness of all things. In a world often fraught with uncertainty and turmoil, spirituality offers a beacon of hope, reminding us that true fulfilment lies not in external achievements but in the richness of our inner landscape.

It's an ever-unfolding path, inviting us to walk with curiosity, compassion, and an open heart. With each step, we draw closer to the essence of our own being and the timeless wisdom that resides within us all. Spirituality transforms our perspective, allowing us to see beyond the surface and connect with the deeper truths of life.

The Path Within

"The way is not in the sky; the way is in the heart." — Buddha

This quote encapsulates the essence of spirituality. It's not about seeking external validation or lofty ideals; it's about turning inward and listening to the wisdom of our hearts. The journey is personal and unique to each individual, yet it is universal in its ability to transform and uplift.

Spirituality invites us to live with intention and purpose, to cultivate a sense of wonder and gratitude for the simple joys of life. It teaches us to be present, to appreciate the beauty of each moment, and to find peace amidst the noise. In doing so, we begin to realize that the true path to happiness and contentment lies within us.

By embracing spirituality, we learn to navigate life with a sense of calm and clarity, grounded in the knowledge that we are part of something greater. This understanding brings a profound sense of peace, where regrets fade, and inner harmony reigns.

The Journey Continues

Spirituality is not a destination but a continuous journey of growth and self-discovery. It encourages us to be kind to ourselves and others, to seek meaning in our experiences, and to live with an open heart. It's a journey of finding balance, where we learn to harmonize our inner world with the outer world.

In this journey, we discover that the most important truths are often the simplest ones. We find that happiness is not about acquiring more but about appreciating what we already have. We learn that love, compassion, and understanding are the keys to a fulfilling life.

In the end, spirituality is about finding our way home to ourselves. It's about uncovering the divine within and recognizing that we are all interconnected. As we walk this path, we bring light into our lives and the lives of those around us.

Conclusion

Spirituality offers a profound and transformative journey, guiding us towards inner peace and fulfilment. It reminds us that true happiness lies not in external achievements but in the richness of our inner landscape. By embracing spirituality with curiosity, compassion, and an open heart, we draw closer to the essence of our own being and the timeless wisdom that resides within us all.

"Spirituality: where regrets fade, and peace reigns."

The white board syndrome

The White Board Syndrome** is not a type of disease but a metaphorical concept I created to highlight the mindset of those who drown in their own sadness and complaints, thereby worsening their lives. This syndrome is common in today's generation, where people often allow their negative thoughts to dominate their reality. Remember, no one can worsen your life unless you give them permission.

What is White Board Syndrome?

White Board Syndrome illustrates how our brains can distort problems, making them appear far worse than they actually are. It's about how we mentally tackle difficult situations, identifying the real issues versus the exaggerated ones created by our minds.

To make this concept clearer, consider the following figures:

FIGURE A: The Original Life

This figure represents the genuine problems a person faces. These problems are real and tangible, but they are manageable.

FIGURE B: The Cloned Life

In this figure, the original problems have been distorted by negative thinking, anxiety, and fear. The person believes these exaggerated problems are their true reality, making their situation seem much worse than it actually is.

Understanding the Impact

When someone suffers from White Board Syndrome, their thinking amplifies the severity of their problems. This distorted perception evolves into anxiety and fear, causing them to live in a "cloned" version of their life—a life filled with exaggerated issues that overshadow their genuine reality.

By understanding this, we can see how important it is to manage our thoughts and perceptions. Recognizing that our minds can create false realities helps us stay grounded and better handle our actual problems.

Breaking Free from White Board Syndrome

To avoid falling victim to White Board Syndrome, practice these steps:

1. Identify the Real Problem: Separate your genuine issues from the exaggerated ones created by your mind.

2. Challenge Negative Thoughts: Question the validity of your fears and anxieties. Are they based on facts or just assumptions?

3. Stay Present: Focus on the present moment instead of dwelling on past regrets or future worries.

4.Seek Support: Talk to friends, family, or a mental health professional to gain perspective.

5. Practice Mindfulness: Engage in mindfulness practices like meditation to help calm your mind and reduce anxiety.

By adopting these practices, you can prevent your thinking from distorting your reality and worsening your situation. Remember, your thoughts have the power to shape your perception, so choose to see your problems as they truly are—not as your mind's exaggerations.

Conclusion

White Board Syndrome serves as a reminder of how our thoughts can manipulate our reality. By understanding and managing our perceptions, we can prevent our minds from creating false problems and live more authentic, peaceful lives.

From now on, don't let White Board Syndrome make you feel sick. Recognize the difference between your real life and the cloned version your mind creates, and focus on maintaining a clear, grounded perspective. See in both fig: A and B

Some Principle's for Living a Great and Happy Life

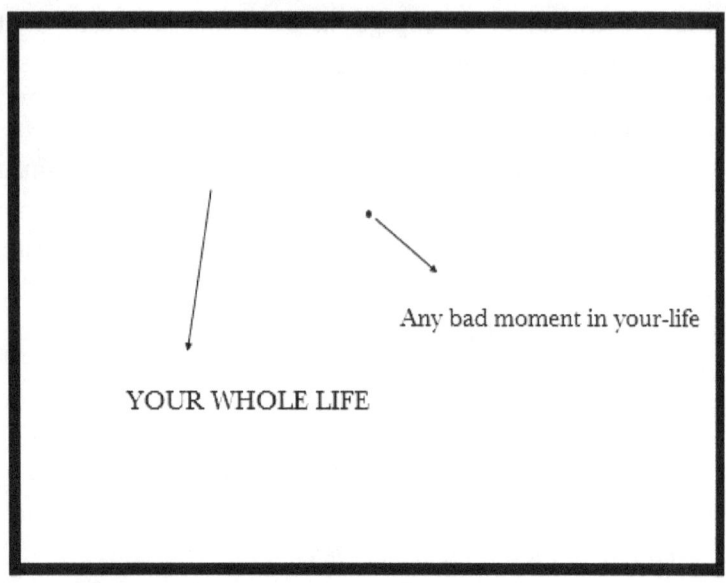

FIG A: THE ORIGINAL LIFE

FIG: B {THE CLONED LIFE}

We can clearly saw that the thinking makes the problem even worse than the real problem we can say thinking evolve the anxiety and fear for that situation which makes you feel that cloned life is your real life not you genuine life so from now never felt sick from "WHITE BOARD SYNDROME".

Overcoming Anxiety: The NPC Technique

Many teens struggle with confidence issues, especially when facing situations like public speaking or taking on significant challenges. This anxiety can manifest as nervousness, panic, and a pervasive sense of dread. Just the thought of speaking in front of others can make your mind race and your heart pound. When someone calls your name and you step onto the stage, the balloon of anxiety bursts, and nervousness floods your brain. However, as you start your speech, things gradually become manageable. But why does this happen? For some, it may seem natural, but for others like me, it feels like a curse. I've missed out on several important events due to anxiety and nervousness. Fortunately, I discovered a method to tackle this: the NPC technique.

What is the NPC Technique?

If you enjoy playing games like Grand Theft Auto (GTA), you're familiar with NPCs (Non-Playable Characters). In the game, NPCs are the characters you interact with, but they don't influence the main storyline—they're just there to create the environment. Applying this concept to real life, the NPC technique can help reduce anxiety and nervousness, boosting your confidence and courage.

How the NPC Technique Works

When I'm about to face a crowd or give a speech, I use the NPC technique. I imagine myself as the main character and everyone else as NPCs. This mindset shift allows me to speak fluently and confidently, as it feels like I'm in control of the situation, just like in a video game. It might sound crazy, but it works! Here's how you can apply it:

1. Imagine You're the Main Character: Visualize yourself as the protagonist of a game. The crowd or audience is filled with NPCs who are part of the environment but not central to your mission.

2. Focus on Your Role: Remind yourself that as the main character, you have a purpose and a message to deliver. The NPCs are there to support your journey, not judge it.

3. Maintain Control: Keep the mindset that you are in control of your narrative. The NPCs cannot derail your story; they are simply part of the background.

Benefits of the NPC Technique

- Reduces Anxiety: Shifting your focus from what others think to your own role reduces the pressure and helps calm your nerves.
- Boosts Confidence: Seeing yourself as the main character empowers you to take charge and perform better.
- Enhances Focus: Concentrating on your mission rather than the audience's reactions keeps you grounded and clear-headed.

Be the Main Character in Your Life

Beyond public speaking, the NPC technique can be a powerful tool for everyday life. Don't let anyone else become the main character in your story. If you allow others to dictate your actions and emotions, you risk losing control of your narrative, leading to a sense of powerlessness and even self-destruction.

Mark my words: **Be the main character in your life**. Don't let anyone else take that role, as it can lead to your downfall. Embrace your story, face your challenges head-on, and remember that the NPCs are just part of the scenery. This mindset will not only help you overcome anxiety but also lead a more confident and fulfilling life.

HEAVY ROCKET

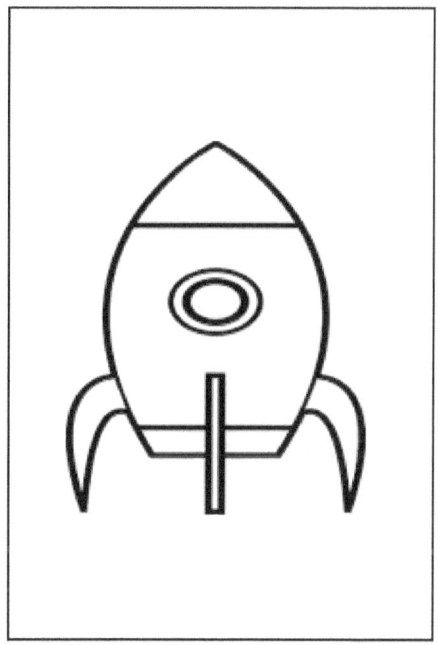

Imagine a heavy rocket, grounded and unable to take off. Analysing this situation, you might think the solution is simple: ignite a fire to create thrust, and the rocket will soar into the sky. But let's delve deeper into what this heavy rocket represents and how we can truly make it fly.

The Heavy Rocket as a Metaphor

This heavy rocket symbolizes your emotional state, burdened with negative affirmations, failures, obstacles, rejection, jealousy, lust, and hate. These elements weigh you down, preventing you from reaching your full potential. Just like a rocket filled with unnecessary weight, your emotional control area becomes clogged with things that hinder your progress.

Steps to Make the Rocket Fly

1. **Identify the Wastage**: Recognize the negative elements in your life. These can be toxic thoughts, harmful relationships, past failures, and emotional baggage.

2. **Deduct the Wastage**: Actively work to remove these negative influences. This might involve changing your thought patterns, seeking closure on past events, and distancing yourself from negative people.

3. **Stock Up on Positive Fuel**: Replace the negativity with positive affirmations, supportive relationships, and constructive habits. Surround yourself with positivity and encouragement.

4. **Ignite the Fire of Positivity**: Use your newfound positivity as the fuel to ignite your rocket. This fire represents your motivation, determination, and the drive to succeed. With positive affirmations and a clear mindset, you can create the necessary thrust to propel yourself forward.

The Journey to the Stars

By lightening your emotional load and igniting the fire of positive affirmations, your heavy rocket can finally take off. This process is not just about removing the negative but also about fostering the positive. It's about transforming your emotional landscape to support your ambitions and dreams.

- **Let Go of Negative Affirmations**: Replace "I can't" with "I can" and "I'm not good enough" with "I am capable."
- **Overcome Failures**: See failures as learning experiences rather than setbacks.
- **Tackle Obstacles**: View obstacles as challenges to overcome, not insurmountable barriers.
- **Handle Rejection**: Understand that rejection is not a reflection of your worth but an opportunity to grow.
- **Avoid Jealousy and Lust**: Focus on your own journey and goals instead of comparing yourself to others.
- **Transform Hate into Compassion**: Cultivate empathy and understanding towards others.

Conclusion

Your heavy rocket, filled with emotional burdens, can be transformed into a vessel of success and achievement. By removing negative influences and igniting the fire of positivity, you can launch yourself towards your goals and aspirations. Remember, the journey to the stars begins with shedding the weight that holds you back and fuelling yourself with positive energy and determination.

Be the main character in your life and don't let anyone else take control. With the right mindset and actions, you and your rocket can reach up to the stars

Some Principle's for Living a Great and Happy Life

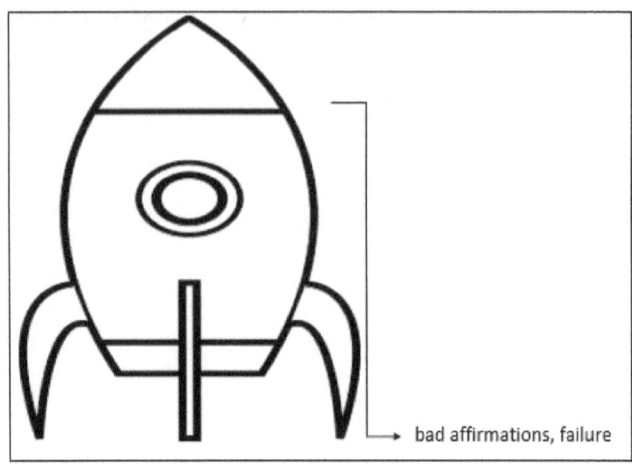

bad affirmations, failure

HIT COIN =>

Hitcoin: The Future of Investing in People

Imagine a world where you could invest in people the same way you invest in stocks, based on their unique strengths and potential for growth. People are like graphs: if you understand how to read them, you can achieve incredible success. The key lies in investing your emotions and efforts in individuals who can offer a high return in terms of valuable connections and meaningful relationships. Introducing **Hitcoin**—a revolutionary concept that helps identify standout individuals in our generation.

The Essence of Hitcoin

Each person is a blend of unique qualities and imperfections. This diversity allows individuals to excel in different areas and achieve greatness in their unique ways. To navigate this complexity and identify exceptional individuals, I've conceptualized Hitcoin—a metaphorical currency that evaluates people based on two fundamental traits:

1. **Creativity**
2. **Consistency**

Understanding Hitcoin

Components of Hitcoin

- **Creativity**: This measures a person's ability to think outside the box, innovate, and approach problems from unique angles. Creative individuals are the ones who bring fresh perspectives and novel solutions.
- **Consistency**: This evaluates how reliably and persistently a person pursues their goals. Consistent individuals are dedicated, hardworking, and capable of maintaining their efforts despite challenges.

Why Hitcoin Matters

Traditional metrics of success, such as grades and standardized test scores, often fail to capture a person's true potential. These conventional measures tend to produce conformists rather than innovators. Hitcoin, on the other hand, focuses on qualities that drive real-world success and personal fulfilment.

Creativity and Consistency Over Conventional Metrics

Hitcoin values creativity and consistency above traditional metrics like grades and test scores. By investing in individuals who excel in these areas, you are more likely to discover future leaders, innovators, and change-makers.

How to Utilize Hitcoin

1. **Identify Creativity**: Look for individuals who demonstrate originality, innovative thinking, and problem-solving skills.

These are the people who come up with ground-breaking ideas and creative solutions.
2. **Evaluate Consistency**: Observe individuals' work ethic, dedication to their goals, and resilience in the face of obstacles. Consistent individuals are those who persistently work towards their aspirations, no matter the challenges.
3. **Invest in People**: Allocate your emotional and professional resources towards individuals with high Hitcoin scores. These are the people most likely to achieve extraordinary things and make significant contributions to their fields.

The Benefits of Hitcoin

High Return on Investment

By focusing on creativity and consistency, Hitcoin allows you to invest in people who will likely provide high returns in terms of personal and professional growth. These investments lead to stronger connections, more meaningful relationships, and a greater impact on your community and beyond.

Transformative Relationships

Investing in individuals with high Hitcoin values leads to transformative relationships. These individuals bring new ideas, drive innovation, and inspire those around them. Your investment in them helps create a ripple effect of positivity and progress.

Conclusion

Hitcoin is a ground-breaking way to evaluate and invest in people. By focusing on creativity and consistency, you can identify individuals with the potential to achieve greatness. In a world where traditional metrics often fall short, Hitcoin offers a fresh and insightful perspective on what it means to be successful.

Embrace the Hitcoin philosophy, and start recognizing the true masterpieces among us. By investing in individuals with high Hitcoin values, you not only enhance your own life but also contribute to a more innovative and compassionate world.

HITCOIN ➜ <u>CREATIVNESS</u>   X=X MARKS

CONSITENCY

Hitcoin is depend in only two factors that how much a person is creative and their consistency in a work it is unequal to marks, all kinds of fucking results that only help to admit slaves

The castle of patience

In today's fast-paced world, patience is a rare virtue. Many people want immediate results and give up on their efforts when they don't see quick success. This lack of patience can lead to abandoned goals and unfulfilled potential. To combat this, I introduce the **Castle of Patience**—a simple yet powerful exercise designed to test and enhance your patience.

The Concept: The Castle of Patience

The Castle of Patience is a metaphorical and practical exercise to build and measure your patience. Imagine constructing a castle out of cards, with each layer representing a level of patience. This exercise not only helps you gauge your current level of patience but also provides a structured way to improve it.

How to Build Your Castle of Patience

1. **Start with a Strong Foundation**: Begin by constructing the first layer of your card castle. This requires steady hands and a calm mind. Focus on each card and place it carefully to create a stable base.

2. **Build Up Layer by Layer**: Continue adding layers to your castle. With each layer, the challenge increases, requiring more focus and patience. Aim to build a castle with 7 layers.

Assessing Your Patience Level

- **7 Layers**: If you can build a 7-layer card castle without losing patience, congratulations! You possess a high level of patience, which is rare and commendable.

- **6 Layers**: Achieving 6 layers is good, but there's room for improvement. Practice regularly to reach the 7-layer mark.

- **5 Layers or Fewer**: If you can only manage 5 layers or fewer, it indicates that your patience needs significant work. Reducing screen time and engaging more with the real world can help you build patience.

Enhancing Your Patience

1. **Practice Regularly**: Make the Castle of Patience a daily or weekly exercise. Each attempt helps strengthen your patience muscle.

2. **Reduce Distractions**: Limit time spent on your phone or other distractions. Engage in activities that require sustained focus and patience, such as reading, gardening, or painting.

3. **Mindfulness and Meditation**: Incorporate mindfulness practices and meditation into your routine. These techniques are proven to enhance patience and overall mental well-being.
4. **Gradual Progression**: Once you master the 7-layer castle, increase the challenge. Aim to build more complex structures, like a beautiful fort, to further test and improve your patience.

The Importance of Patience

Patience is a crucial trait for achieving long-term success and happiness. It allows you to:

- **Persist Through Challenges**: With patience, you can endure setbacks and keep working towards your goals.
- **Improve Skills**: Patience enables you to take the time needed to hone your abilities and achieve mastery.
- **Build Better Relationships**: Patient individuals tend to have stronger, more meaningful relationships because they are better listeners and more understanding.

Conclusion

The Castle of Patience is more than just a card-building exercise—it's a pathway to personal growth and success. By practicing and enhancing your patience, you set yourself up for greater achievements and a more fulfilling life. Start building your castle today, and watch your patience—and your potential—grow.

Remember brother in today's world everything has a cost literally everything at one certain point every person sells thyself "EVERYTHING HAS A COST" even in today's world you can now buy an human they are now for sale so earn the real shit. whereas some things that are not buyable has also a cost:

"PATIENCE IS THE COST OF LOVE."

"DEATH IS THE COST OF LIFE."

"AGE IS THE COST OF DEATH."

"DEVOTION IS THE COST OF PARADISE"

"ANXIETY IS THE COST OF AGE"

"HAPPINESS IS THE COST OF SADNESS"

"JOY IS THE COST OF PAIN"

In the currency of life, everything comes with a price tag. Every decision, every action, every emotion exacts its toll. It's a harsh reality we face: "EVERYTHING HAS A COST." But delve deeper, and you'll find that some costs are not measured in dollars and cents; they're paid in the currency of the soul.

The Price of Existence

- "PATIENCE IS THE COST OF LOVE.": To truly love someone, we must endure the trials of time with unwavering patience. It's the price we pay for the deep connection and intimacy that love brings.
- "DEATH IS THE COST OF LIFE.": Life is a journey with an inevitable destination. Death, the final toll, reminds us of the fragility and preciousness of existence.
- "AGE IS THE COST OF DEATH.": As time passes, we grow older, inching closer to our inevitable end. Age, the toll of existence, marks the passage of time and the cycle of life.

The Sacrifices We Make

- **"DEVOTION IS THE COST OF PARADISE."**: To attain paradise, whether in this life or the next, we must devote ourselves wholly to a cause or belief. It's the price we pay for the ultimate reward.
- **"ANXIETY IS THE COST OF AGE."**: With age comes wisdom, but also anxiety. The weight of responsibilities and uncertainties increases as we journey through life.

The Balance of Emotions

- **"HAPPINESS IS THE COST OF SADNESS."**: The peaks of joy are often preceded by valleys of sadness. It's the contrast of emotions that makes happiness all the more precious.
- **"JOY IS THE COST OF PAIN."**: Pain, whether physical or emotional, makes us appreciate the moments of joy and bliss. It's the contrast of experiences that gives depth to our lives.

Conclusion: The Price We Pay

In the grand exchange of life, every experience, every feeling, every moment carries its own cost. It's the currency of existence, the ledger of our journey. But amidst the transactions, amidst the sacrifices and tribulations, we find meaning. For it's in paying the price that we truly understand the value of what we gain. So let us embrace the costs, for they are the currency of growth, of wisdom, of life itself.

THE UMANG FORMULA

U - Understanding and Empathy:

- Seek to understand others and show empathy. Strong relationships are built on mutual respect and the ability to see the world through another's eyes

M - Mindfulness and Presence:

- Practice mindfulness by being fully present in the moment. This reduces stress and increases happiness by preventing worry about the past or future.

A - Aspiration and Achievement:

- Set clear goals and work towards them with determination. Celebrate your achievements, no matter how small, as each is a step towards your aspirations.

N - Nourishment of Body and Mind:

- Take care of your physical health through exercise and a balanced diet. Equally, nourish your mind with positive thoughts and continuous learning.

G - Generosity and Gratitude:

- Live generously, giving your time, resources, and kindness without expecting anything in return. Cultivate gratitude for what you have, rather than focusing on what you lack.

This formula is a guide to living a life that is rich in personal growth, health, and meaningful connections. It's about understanding the balance between giving and receiving, and recognizing the importance of both mental and physical well-being. I hope you like "UMANG" formula.

Be like time

Here in this context, I am not telling about what time is how it works here I am going to share some principle's that I learn from time:

1. Mercy: when there was something bad happens to me then after it the moments getting more worse and worse life and time shows no mercy to anyone don't show mercy on thyself, I guess how David Goggin's became the world strongest man.
2. Don't stop: time never stops for anyone it goes and goes I think that is why people respect so much of time. time comes to every person but in a limited quantity some of you wasted it and some utilise it. don't stop keep going on the path.

Trust meter:

Trust, once a cherished commodity, has become commonplace in today's era. Despite the prevalence of claims like "I trust you," the reality is often far from it. But fear not, for I present to you a quirky yet insightful technique to gauge someone's trustworthiness: **THE ICE**.

Yes, you read that right—the ice. Now, before you dismiss it as absurd, consider this: How long would you keep your hand submerged in ice? 10 minutes? 20? 30? Let's say an hour. Now, imagine removing your hand from the ice. Just as the cold numbs your hand, trust can sometimes leave us feeling numb too.

The Ice Technique: Testing Trust

Here's how it works:

1. **The Ice Test**: Just like enduring the chill of ice, entrusting someone with our trust can be both uncomfortable and risky. But, much like the ice, trust can melt away unexpectedly.

2. **Be Cold Like Ice**: To assess someone's trustworthiness, metaphorically leave the connection and adopt a cold, indifferent stance. Stop caring, stop investing emotionally, and observe who sticks around and who drifts away.
3. **The Revealing Thaw**: As you withdraw your warmth and affection, watch closely. Those who remain steadfast, even in the absence of your trust, are the ones worthy of your confidence. They weather the frost and remain by your side.

The Lesson of the Ice

The Ice technique may sound unconventional, but its message is clear: Trust is fragile, much like ice. It requires careful handling and can easily melt away if mishandled. By embracing the coldness of the ice, we gain clarity on who truly deserves our trust and loyalty.

So, the next time you're unsure about someone's trustworthiness, remember the ice. Take a step back, observe, and let their actions speak louder than words. After all, in a world where trust is often taken for granted, it's essential to have a reliable method to separate the true friends from the fleeting acquaintances.

The last option

Embarking on a journey of self-discovery and growth requires dedication, perseverance, and a willingness to challenge oneself. If you find yourself at a crossroads, unsure of your next steps in career or personal development, fear not. I present to you a transformative formula divided into two distinct phases, designed to reshape your mindset, strengthen your connections, and unlock your full potential.

In the initial phase, you'll lay the groundwork for personal growth by embracing discomfort and building resilience. Here's what to focus on:

1. **Embrace Solitude**: Cut off external distractions and learn to be comfortable in your own company. Silence cultivates introspection and self-awareness.

2. **Master Self-Control**: Challenge yourself to abstain from distractions like social media and pornography. Redirect your energy towards productive pursuits that nurture your mind and body.

3. **Cultivate Silence**: Practice the art of silence, allowing your thoughts to settle and your inner voice to emerge. Stillness fosters clarity and insight.

4. **Expand Your Mind**: Immerse yourself in literature, exploring diverse perspectives and expanding your intellectual horizons. Reading stimulates imagination and empathy.

5. **Nurture Spirituality**: Connect with your spiritual side, whether through meditation, prayer, or mindfulness practices. Spiritual growth nourishes the soul and provides inner strength.

6. **Engage Your Imagination**: Explore the world of cinema, seeking out thought-provoking films that challenge your perceptions and ignite your creativity.

7. **Prioritize Physical Health**: Dedicate time to exercise, strengthening both body and mind. Physical fitness boosts confidence and resilience.

8. **Pursue Knowledge**: Develop a thirst for knowledge, seeking to understand the world and your place within it. Lifelong learning fuels personal growth and self-discovery.

Phase Two: Integration and Expansion (Next 4 Months)

Having fortified your foundation, it's time to step out of your comfort zone and forge meaningful connections. Here's how to proceed:

1. **Embrace Socialization**: Reconnect with others and cultivate new relationships. Human connection nourishes the soul and provides support during times of adversity.
2. **Expand Your Network**: Challenge yourself to engage with new people daily, both online and offline. Each interaction offers an opportunity for growth and learning.
3. **Embrace Extroversion**: Step into the role of an extrovert, embracing social interactions and seeking out new experiences. Boldness opens doors to new opportunities.
4. **Foster Genuine Connections**: Cultivate authentic friendships based on mutual respect and understanding. Surround yourself with individuals who inspire and uplift you.
5. **Transition from Fiction to Reality**: Transition from the realm of novels to the complexities of real-life interactions. Apply the lessons learned from literature to navigate the intricacies of human relationships.

The Essence of the Formula

This formula is not merely a prescription for personal growth; it's a roadmap to self-discovery and fulfilments. By immersing yourself in solitude, expanding your mind, nurturing relationships, and embracing new experiences, you'll undergo a profound transformation. Remember, growth requires patience, perseverance, and a willingness to step outside your comfort zone. Trust in the process, and watch as your potential unfolds before you.

ENHANCE IT MORE MAKE IT FULLER OF INFORMATIONS AND INTERESTING TO READ

A cleaned life

In my life a very strange phenomenon usually happened when I am scolded by my parent I kind a hate them and when my parents do the good things for me I started to love them but why I am sure it all happens to you and that's why you used to live in a good books of PEOPLES no matter in further your result get worse sometimes to you are unable to say no to people thinks if I said no maybe he/she started to hate me but ask a question to yourself not today but someday you have to say no to them you can't say always yes for their work not always wreck your time . people's life are life a cotton white pure cotton if anyone spilt the black ink it spread and after it becomes bad people are always wanted to be best always wanted to be in a good-books of people

Some Principle's for Living a Great and Happy Life

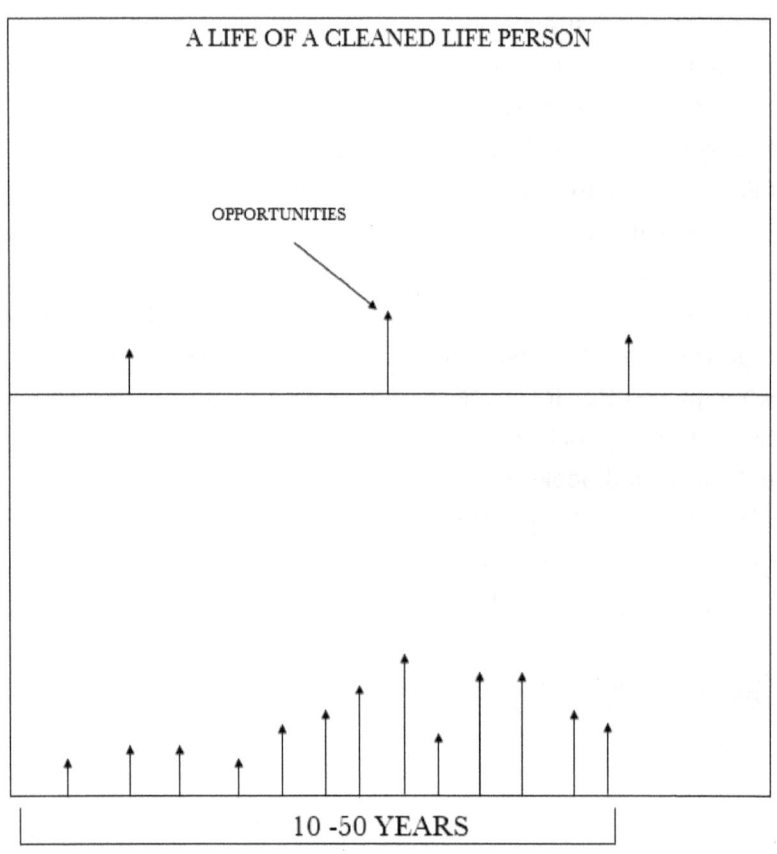

FIG: A

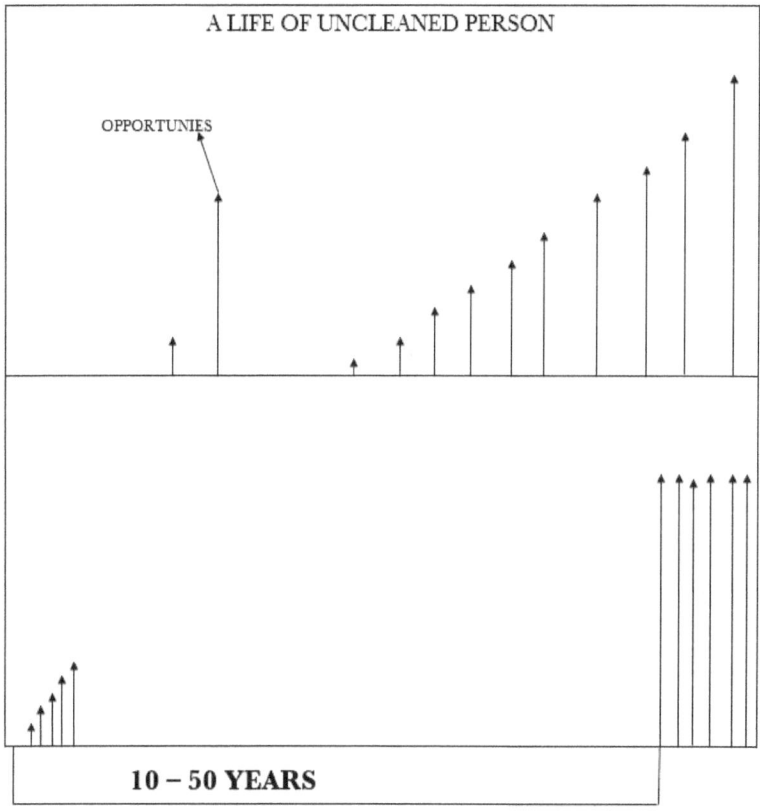

FIG: B

Ah, the intricate dance of emotions and expectations! Your observation about how our feelings toward others can shift dramatically based on their actions resonates with many of us. It's like riding an emotional rollercoaster, isn't it?

Let's break down your thought-provoking musings and explore the delicate balance between saying "yes" and "no," the dynamics of relationships, and the opportunities that unfold over time.

The Yes-No Conundrum

When it comes to saying "yes" or "no," it's like navigating a maze. Sometimes we're caught in the web of politeness, fearing that a refusal might strain our relationships. But here's the truth: **saying "no" doesn't make you a villain; it makes you a guardian of your time and energy.**

The Good-Books Illusion

In Figure A, we see the person who lives perpetually in the good-books of others. They're the "yes" people, always accommodating, always eager to please. Their opportunities are like rare gems—few and far between. But what happens when they're stretched thin, their time rented out to everyone else? When they need help, the renters vanish like smoke.

The Real-Life Trailblazer

Now, let's turn our attention to Figure B. This person doesn't always fit the mould of "good-books material." They've learned the art of saying "no." Initially, they may have wrecked some time, but eventually, they discovered the magic of boundaries.

- **They invest their working years wisely**, focusing on personal growth, learning, and building skills.
- **When they need renters**, they find a bustling marketplace. Their "no" has become a powerful currency, exchanged for opportunities, collaborations, and meaningful connections.

The Cotton of Life

Your cotton analogy is spot-on! Life starts as pristine white cotton, untainted by ink. But as we journey through it, we encounter both black and colourful inks.

- **Black Ink**: These are the challenges, setbacks, and disappointments—the moments when we say "no" to ourselves or others. They spread, leaving stains. But guess what? These stains shape us, teach us resilience, and add depth to our fabric.
- **Colourful Inks**: These represent our passions, dreams, and positive experiences—the moments when we say "yes" to growth, love, and adventure. They infuse vibrancy into our cotton.

The Critique and Forgetfulness

You're absolutely right. People have short memories when it comes to kindness. They might forget the good things you've done, but they'll remember the one time you said "no." It's like they've got a selective memory filter!

So, here's the takeaway:

- **Say "no" when it matters.** Protect your time, sanity, and dreams.
- **Be in your own good books.** Prioritize your well-being over external validation.
- **Embrace the ink stains.** They're part of your unique tapestry.
- **Remember that life's cotton is yours to weave.** Choose your colours wisely.

And hey, if life were a colouring book, I'd say you're creating a masterpiece! Keep saying "yes" to growth, and don't hesitate to wield that "no" when needed. You're the artist of your own story!

Now, let's sprinkle some humour into this serious discussion. Why did the "yes" person become a doormat? Because they couldn't say "no" to anyone, and now they're flat!

Feel free to ask for more stories, quotes, or insights—I'm here to weave them into your cotton canvas!

Anger zone = danger zone

We all are trapped in a cycle of life and death, roaming for eternal years through countless lifetimes. In every life, we experience a mixture of pain and happiness. But there is one crucial aspect that is within our control: whether we choose to suffer from our emotions or not. Unfortunately, we often choose to let anger take hold of us, leading to our own suffering.

In Jainism, anger (known as "krodh") is considered one of the most harmful emotions. It not only affects us in this life but also leaves a lasting impact on our future lives. Anger is like riding your favourite bike, which represents your one precious life. When you accelerate [anger], you reach top speed [anger on top of your head]. At this point, there are two possible outcomes: either you crash, or you somehow manage to stay safe.

If you crash, your anger has destroyed you. Even if you don't crash, the damage has already been done to your bike [life]. The repercussions of anger are inevitable. No one can deny the existence of anger, but we must strive to control it rather than letting it control us.

When we are consumed by anger, we lose our true sight and often do things we later regret. Anger clouds our judgment, leading us to act in ways that are harmful to ourselves and others. We say things we don't mean, make decisions we wouldn't normally make, and behave in ways that are contrary to our true nature. In this state, we not only cause pain to those around us but also accumulate negative karma that affects our future lives.

Lord Mahavir, the 24th Tirthankara in Jainism, wisely said, "Anger begets more anger, and forgiveness and love lead to more forgiveness and love." This profound teaching highlights the cyclical nature of our emotions. Anger breeds more anger, creating a vicious cycle of negativity. On the other hand, forgiveness and love generate more forgiveness and love, fostering a positive and peaceful cycle.

To break free from the cycle of anger, we must practice self-awareness and mindfulness. Recognize the triggers of anger and consciously choose to respond with calmness and understanding. It is not an easy task, but with consistent effort, we can learn to control our anger rather than being controlled by it.

Imagine the peace and happiness that can be achieved by letting go of anger. By choosing forgiveness and love, we not only improve our current life but also create a better foundation for our future lives. We can transform the anger zone into a zone of peace and positivity, benefiting ourselves and everyone around us.

In conclusion, anger is a dangerous emotion that can lead to destructive consequences. It blinds us, causes us to act irrationally, and damages our lives. However, by following the teachings of Lord Mahavir and striving to control our anger, we can break free from its grip. Let us choose forgiveness and love, creating a cycle of positivity that will enhance our lives and the lives of those around us. Remember, the anger zone is a danger zone, but with mindfulness and effort, we can transform it into a zone of peace and harmony.

Conclusion

This enriching exploration unveiled the transformative power of cultivating a "growth mindset." We charted a path towards enduring success, reframing challenges as stepping stones — catalysts that propel us forward on our odyssey to mastery. By internalizing the belief that our abilities are not fixed but can be developed through deliberate practice, we foster a growth mindset. This empowering perspective stands in stark contrast to a "fixed mindset," which views intelligence and talent as innate and unchangeable.

The S.M.A.R.T. goal framework serves as a compass, guiding us in translating aspirations into actionable steps. It equips us to set Specific, Measurable, Achievable, Relevant, and Time-Bound goals, bridging the chasm between dreams and achievements. Patience emerges as the cornerstone of this success formula. The "Castle of Patience" exercise fortifies our determination to persevere in the face of adversity, reminding us that significant achievements are often the product of sustained effort over time. As we seamlessly integrate these principles into the fabric of our being, we unlock the doorway to our boundless potential.

Embarking on a transformative voyage of self-discovery and fulfilment, we become the architects of our own success stories. This journey, however, is not a linear sprint but a meandering exploration, complete with its own detours and roadblocks. Patience is our compass, guiding us through uncharted territories. There will be moments of frustration and self-doubt, but the unwavering belief in our potential serves as our guiding star. As we celebrate milestones and navigate setbacks, we refine our approach, our resilience bolstered by each experience. With unwavering dedication and a growth mindset, we transform into the architects of our destinies, etching our stories onto the grand canvas of life.

Furthermore, cultivating a growth mindset empowers us to embrace challenges with enthusiasm. We learn to view them as opportunities to stretch our abilities and refine our skills. This newfound perspective fosters a love of learning, propelling us to continuously seek out knowledge and expand our horizons. As we confront obstacles, we develop a tenacious spirit, continually striving to improve and conquer new frontiers.

The journey towards self-mastery is a lifelong pursuit, enriched by moments of triumph and coloured by periods of struggle. Yet, with unwavering dedication and a growth mindset, we can transform these challenges into stepping stones on our path to excellence. By embracing lifelong learning and fostering a love of exploration, we become the architects of our destinies, forever etching our unique stories onto the grand tapestry of human experience.

Embarking on this odyssey of self-discovery equips us with the tools to navigate the inevitable roadblocks that arise along the way. The growth mindset empowers us to reframe setbacks as temporary hurdles, fostering resilience in the face of adversity. Patience becomes our compass, guiding us through uncharted territories and reminding us that significant accomplishments are often the product of sustained effort over time. As we confront challenges, we cultivate a tenacious spirit, continually striving to improve and rewrite the narrative of our limitations.

Moreover, a growth mindset fosters a love of learning, intrinsically motivating us to continuously expand our knowledge and refine our skills. We embrace challenges with curiosity, viewing them as opportunities to experiment and step outside our comfort zones. This insatiable desire for knowledge fuels our lifelong journey of exploration, propelling us to new heights of achievement.

The path to self-mastery is not a solitary expedition; it is a collaborative endeavour enriched by the support and guidance of others. Sharing our experiences and challenges with mentors and peers fosters a sense of community and belonging. By drawing inspiration from the successes of others and offering support during their times of struggle, we collectively chart a course towards shared triumphs. As we learn from and collaborate with others, we refine our approach, our collective wisdom illuminating the path forward.

When you grow up you start to understand life is not easy as you understand in your early life. life is a full complete package of happiness, sadness, fear and much more but in life's package god sent every quantity of every component equal but we think in my life there is no sign of happiness. Only there were bundle of sadness, anxiety and lil bit of depression but as I said your mindset is fixed make a growth mindset your life change the tracks. hope you like this part we will meet you in next part.

This generation often finds itself lost in their phones, absorbed by the endless streams of information and entertainment. While some may discover fragments of wisdom through this medium, they might not realize there is an ocean of wisdom available to them. This profound insight comes from engaging with their older selves—particularly their grandparents. Talking to them, or even just listening to their stories and experiences, can provide a deep reservoir of knowledge and perspective that can't be found on a screen. Embrace these conversations and allow the wisdom of previous generations to enrich your life.

In the end, it's simple: **Mindset shapes destiny**. The digital generation, Gen-Z, holds the power to innovate and inspire. By choosing hope over expectation and **patience over haste**, we can cultivate a life of meaning. Embrace the quiet strength of spirituality to navigate through life's noise. Remember, true wealth lies in our thoughts and actions, not in our wallets. **As the Dalai Lama wisely said, "Happiness is not something ready-made. It comes from your own actions."**

PART- 4

Start From Scratch

Boarding on a new journey can be both exhilarating and daunting. "Start from Scratch" is a chapter dedicated to the brave souls who dare to begin a new, to those who are not afraid to reset their lives and build from the ground up.

In this chapter, we will dive into the stories of individuals who have faced the blank canvas of possibility and chose to create masterpieces. We will explore the courage it takes to start from zero, the resilience required to face unforeseen challenges, and the satisfaction that comes from watching your efforts take shape.

Whether it's a new career, a new relationship, or a new adventure, starting from scratch means embracing the unknown with open arms. It's about trusting the process, learning from each step, and growing stronger with every stumble.

So, let's turn the page and begin this adventure together. May the stories within inspire you to take that leap of faith, to believe in your ability to start from scratch, and to recognize that every end is just the beginning of something new.

Starting Fresh

Every journey begins with a single step. And sometimes, the hardest part is just that — starting. But here's the thing: **every day is a new chance to begin again**. So, let's take that chance together and embark on a journey of self-improvement.

Understanding Yourself

Before we can improve, we need to understand who we are. Take a moment to reflect on your thoughts, feelings, and actions. Ask yourself:

- What makes me happy?

- What am I good at?
- What do I want to change?

Setting Goals

Now that you know more about yourself, it's time to set some goals. Remember, goals should be:

- **Specific**: Clearly define what you want to achieve. work for that!!
- **Measurable**: How will you know when you've achieved it?
- **Achievable**: Make sure it's something you can realistically accomplish. Not like angels and mermaid.
- **Relevant**: It should matter to you and align with your values.
- **Time-bound**: Set a deadline to keep yourself on track. Without deadline your procrastination will eat your aim.

Taking Action

With your goals set, it's time to act. Break down your goals into small, manageable steps. Then, start with the easiest task don't do the hardest first because you are starting from scratch means you are beginner also a lost one by completing the easiest one it will give you the confidence to tackle the next one.

Staying Positive

On this journey, you'll face challenges. That's okay. It's part of the process. When things get tough, stay positive. Remember why you started and how far you've come. And stay away the peoples who shares you negative and dull vibe.

Celebrating Success as well as failure

Every small victory is worth celebrating but it does not mean you never failed when you failed you remember the mistake that you made it before so the probability of success gets increased so embrace failure too.

Reflecting and Adjusting

As you progress, take time to reflect. What's working? What's not? Adjust your approach as needed. Self-improvement is a continuous process, not a one-time event. Chance and make it on your own track.

Embracing Change

Change can be scary, but it's also exciting. It means you're growing. Embrace it. Be proud of yourself for having the courage to change. Also, one thing I learns in life some changes make a path to success short. But every turn you drop your favourite thing behind that's why success does not come to everyone.

Continuing the Journey

Self-improvement doesn't have an end. It's a lifelong journey. Keep learning, growing, and becoming the best version of yourself.

Remember, **you are capable of amazing things**. Just take it one step at a time. Good luck on your journey! And remember always life and time is not merciful. So, make your choices great after that you don't regret.

When you start something from scratch you gain every detailed knowledge of that thing and if you move forward the amount of knowledge increases with every drop you can make your own ocean.

"**Never too old, never too bad, never too late, never too sick to start from scratch once again—Bikram Choudhary.**

Conclusion:

So, we're at the end of our "Start from Scratch" chapter. It's been quite a ride, hasn't it? Starting from scratch is all about being brave. It's about stepping into the unknown and saying, "I can do this."

Remember, every day is a new chance to start over. Made a mistake? That's okay. Mistakes are our best teachers. They show us where we went wrong and how we can do better next time.

And here's the exciting part: starting from scratch means you get to build something that's all yours. It's like painting on a blank canvas. You get to choose the colours, the shapes, everything. It's all up to you.

So, as we close this chapter, ask yourself: "What will I create when I start from scratch?" The answer to that question could be the start of an amazing journey. So, go ahead. Take that first step. You've got this!

And always include one thing in your life that you start that thing from scratch whether it is painting, dancing, singing etc. we will meet in another part.

PART- 5

Diverse Personality

Personality is the thing which you can use to change ourself help our mindset to change but we first understand about what personality means we can simply say that it is like mindset but there it contains some traits which makes you different from others .but why I add this part in this book remember a remote car doesn't work without their remote as well as think mindset is a car and personality is your remote the way you makes shift in personality the perspective mindset change personality of a person plays a very prominent role in their life and recognizing your personality is the first way to change yourself and then developing diverse personality In yourself is the second path and then last and most important learn to switch your personality's according to internet there are total 16 types of personalities there are total 8 main types of personality which combines to form a full personality of people.

Extraversion (E), Sensing (S), Thinking (T), Judgment (J), Introversion (I), Intuition (N), Feeling (F), and Perception (P). Socionics divides people into 16 different types, called sociotypes which are; ESTJ, ENTJ, ESFJ, ENFJ, ISTJ, ISFJ, INTJ, INFJ, ESTP, ESFP, ENTP, ENFP, ISTP, ISFP, INTP & INFP.

Architect (INTJ)

Introverted: Architects are introspective and recharge by spending time alone. They value their inner world of thoughts and ideas.

Intuitive: They rely on intuition and patterns to understand complex situations. They see the big picture and connect the dots.

Thinking: Architects make decisions based on logic and reason. Emotions take a back seat.

Judging: They prefer structure, planning, and organization. Spontaneity isn't their style.

Key Traits:

Curious Minds: Architects love learning and exploring. They're like intellectual detectives, always seeking knowledge. think outside the box. Originality matters more than fitting in.

Driven Achievers: Architects set ambitious goals and work tirelessly to achieve them. They're strategic and focused.

Lone Wolves: They're comfortable working alone. Teamwork is fine, but they thrive independently.

In a Nutshell:

Imagine a brilliant scientist designing intricate blueprints for a futuristic city. That's the Architect—analytical, innovative, and determined. They build their own path, even if it means going against the crowd. Architects excel in planning, problem-solving, and envisioning the future. If you meet one, you might just witness a masterpiece in progress.

Logician [INTP]

Introverted: Logicians are like cosy introverts who recharge by spending time alone. They're thoughtful and reflective.

Intuitive: They're like puzzle solvers. Logicians see patterns, connections, and hidden meanings in everything.

Thinking: Logic rules their decisions. Emotions take a back seat—like a robot with a heart.

Perceiving: Logicians are flexible and open-minded. They adapt to new information and explore endless possibilities.

Key Traits:

Curious Minds: Logicians ask "why" a lot. They dissect ideas, theories, and systems to understand how they work.

Creative Innovators: They invent new solutions and theories. Their minds are like bubbling cauldrons of ideas.

Independent Explorers: Logicians explore uncharted territories. They're not afraid to challenge norms.

Abstract Thinkers: Concrete reality is just one layer. Logicians dive into abstract concepts and theories.

In a Nutshell:

Imagine a quirky scientist lost in thought, scribbling equations on a chalkboard. That's the Logician—curious, inventive, and a bit eccentric. They're the mad geniuses behind ground-breaking discoveries.

Commander (ENTJ)

Extroverted: Commanders thrive in social settings. They're like energized extroverts who gain strength from interactions.

Intuitive: They see the bigger picture. Commanders connect the dots and envision grand strategies.

Thinking: Logic guides their decisions. They're like strategic chess players, always planning their next move.

Judging: Commanders love order and efficiency. They're decisive and organized.

Key Traits:

Natural Leaders: Commanders take charge. They're CEOs, generals, and team captains. Their charisma inspires others.

Strategic Planners: They map out goals and execute with precision. Efficiency is their middle name.

Bold Decision-Makers: Commanders don't hesitate. They trust their gut and act swiftly.

Visionaries: They see possibilities beyond the horizon. Commanders build empires, both metaphorically and sometimes literally.

In a Nutshell:

Imagine a confident CEO orchestrating a company's growth. That's the Commander—assertive, visionary, and ready to conquer challenges. Commanders excel in leadership, strategy, and turning dreams into reality. If you meet one, prepare for a dynamic conversation!

Debater (ENTP)

Extroverted: Debaters thrive on social interactions. They're like energetic extroverts who recharge by being around people.

Intuitive: They see possibilities everywhere. Debaters connect ideas, theories, and concepts effortlessly.

Thinking: Logic guides their decisions. Emotions take a back seat—like a curious scientist in a lab coat.

Perceiving: Debaters are adaptable and open-minded. They love exploring new paths.

Key Traits:

Curious Minds: Debater's question everything. They're like curious kids who never stop asking "why."

Creative Innovators: They invent new solutions and theories. Their minds are like brainstorming sessions on steroids.

Challengers: Debaters love a good debate. They'll argue for fun, even if they secretly agree with you.

Big-Picture Thinkers: Details? Nah. Debaters focus on the grand scheme of things.

In a Nutshell:

Imagine a witty philosopher at a lively dinner party, sparking debates and laughing uproariously. That's the Debater—sharp, inventive, and always up for a mental joust. Debaters excel in brainstorming, problem-solving, and turning conversations into intellectual adventures. If you meet one, buckle up for a wild ride!

Advocate (INFJ)

Introverted: Advocates recharge by spending time alone. They're like cosy introverts who value deep connections.

Intuitive: They see beyond the surface. Advocates sense hidden meanings and emotions.

Feeling: Empathy guides their decisions. They're like compassionate counsellors, always considering others' feelings.

Judging: Advocates seek harmony and purpose. They're organized dreamers.

Key Traits:

Empathetic Souls: Advocates feel others' pain. They're like emotional sponges, absorbing the world's struggles.

Visionaries: They dream big. Advocates envision a better world and work toward it.

Quiet Leaders: Advocates lead by example. Their impact ripples quietly but profoundly.

Creative Idealists: They blend imagination with compassion. Advocates write poetry, paint emotions, and heal hearts.

In a Nutshell:

Imagine a gentle artist creating a masterpiece that moves hearts. That's the Advocate—intuitive, caring, and quietly powerful. Advocates excel in understanding others, inspiring change, and leaving a positive mark. If you meet one, cherish their rare magic!

Mediator (INFP)

Introverted: Mediators recharge by spending time alone. They're like cosy introverts who seek inner harmony.

Intuitive: They see beyond the surface. Mediator's sense hidden meanings, emotions, and possibilities.

Feeling: Empathy guides their decisions. They're like compassionate artists, painting emotions with their hearts.

Perceiving: Mediators embrace spontaneity. They flow with life's currents.

Key Traits:

Empathetic Dreamers: Mediators feel deeply. They're like emotional poets, capturing life's beauty and pain.

Idealists: They envision a better world. Mediators fight for justice, kindness, and authenticity.

Creative Souls: Mediators write, paint, and compose. Their art reflects their inner landscapes.

Harmony Seekers: They mend broken hearts and bridge gaps. Mediators are the peacemakers.

In a Nutshell:

Imagine a gentle musician strumming a heartfelt melody. That's the Mediator—introspective, compassionate, and attuned to life's whispers. Mediators excel in understanding emotions, inspiring others, and creating beauty. If you meet one, cherish their quiet magic!

Protagonist (ENFJ)

Extroverted: Protagonists thrive in social settings. They're like friendly extroverts who gain energy from connecting with others.

Intuitive: They see beyond the surface. Protagonists sense emotions, motivations, and hidden meanings.

Feeling: Empathy guides their decisions. They're like compassionate leaders, considering the impact on people.

Judging: Protagonists seek harmony and purpose. They're organized visionaries.

Key Traits:

Natural Leaders: Protagonists inspire others. They're like charismatic coaches, rallying the team.

Empathetic Advocates: They fight for causes. Protagonists champion justice, equality, and positive change.

Creative Optimists: Protagonists envision a better world. Their enthusiasm is contagious.

Harmony-Seekers: They mend relationships and build bridges. Protagonists are the glue that holds communities together.

In a Nutshell:

Imagine a passionate teacher inspiring student to believe in themselves. That's the Protagonist—warm, caring, and ready to make a difference. Protagonists excel in leadership, empathy, and creating a positive impact. If you meet one, you're in for an uplifting experience.

Campaigner (ENFP)

Extroverted: Campaigners thrive on social interactions. They're like enthusiastic extroverts who light up a room.

Intuitive: They see beyond the ordinary. Campaigner's sense hidden possibilities, connections, and excitement.

Feeling: Empathy guides their decisions. They're like compassionate artists, painting emotions with vibrant colours.

Perceiving: Campaigners embrace spontaneity. They dance to life's rhythm.

Key Traits:

Creative Dreamers: Campaigners imagine new worlds. They're like daydreamers with a splash of magic.

Champions of Causes: They fight for justice and equality. Campaigners rally others to make a difference.

Eternal Optimists: Campaigners see silver linings even in stormy clouds. Their positivity is contagious.

Free Spirits: They explore uncharted paths. Campaigners follow their hearts, not just the map.

In a Nutshell:

Imagine a passionate storyteller weaving tales around a campfire. That's the Campaigner—inspiring, warm, and ready to explore life's mysteries. Campaigners excel in creativity, empathy, and sparking joy. If you meet one, prepare for an adventure.

Logistician (ISTJ)

Introverted: Logisticians recharge by spending time alone. They're like cosy introverts who value practicality.

Sensing: They focus on facts and details. Logisticians see the world through a clear lens.

Thinking: Logic guides their decisions. Emotions take a back seat—like a precise engineer.

Judging: Logisticians love order and structure. They're organized problem-solvers.

Key Traits:

Reliable Planners: Logisticians create schedules and stick to them. They're like human calendars.

Duty-Driven: They fulfil responsibilities diligently. Logisticians keep the wheels turning.

Practical Realists: Logisticians deal with reality. Dreams are nice, but they prefer practical solutions.

Loyal Guardians: They protect traditions and honour commitments. Logisticians are the steady rocks.

In a Nutshell:

Imagine a meticulous librarian organizing books on the shelves. That's the Logistician—dependable, methodical, and quietly essential. Logisticians excel in reliability, planning, and keeping things running smoothly. If you meet one, appreciate their steady reliability.

Defender (ISFJ)

Introverted: Defenders recharge by spending time alone. They're like cosy introverts who value stability.

Sensing: They focus on practical details. Defenders see the world through a clear lens.

Feeling: Empathy guides their decisions. They're like compassionate caretakers, always considering others' needs.

Judging: Defenders love structure and tradition. They're reliable and dependable.

Key Traits:

Loyal Protectors: Defenders fiercely guard their loved ones. They're like steadfast knights defending the castle.

Hard Workers: They diligently fulfil responsibilities. Defenders keep things running smoothly behind the scenes.

Practical Realists: Defenders deal with reality. They prefer tried-and-true methods over risky adventures.

Kind Hearts: They quietly support others. Defenders are the reliable friends who listen and care.

In a Nutshell:

Imagine a nurturing librarian organizing books with a gentle smile. That's the Defender—loyal, practical, and always there when you need them. Defenders excel in reliability, compassion, and creating a stable environment. If you meet one, appreciate their quiet strength.

Executive (ESTJ)

Extroverted: Executives thrive in social settings. They're like outgoing organizers who gain energy from interacting with others.

Sensing: They focus on practical details. Executives see the world through a clear lens.

Thinking: Logic guides their decisions. Emotions take a back seat—like efficient project managers.

Judging: Executives love structure and order. They're decisive and reliable.

Key Traits:

Natural Leaders: Executives take charge. They're like CEOs, ensuring everything runs smoothly.

Practical Planners: They create schedules and stick to them. Executives are the ultimate organizers.

Duty-Driven: Executives fulfil responsibilities diligently. They're the backbone of many teams.

Loyal Guardians: They protect traditions and honour commitments. Executives keep things stable.

In a Nutshell:

Imagine a no-nonsense manager orchestrating a successful event. That's the Executive—efficient, dependable, and ready to lead. Executives excel in leadership, organization, and getting things done. If you meet one, appreciate their practical wisdom.

Consul (ESFJ)

Extroverted: Consuls thrive in social settings. They're like friendly extroverts who gain energy from connecting with others.

Sensing: They focus on practical details. Consuls see the world through a clear lens.

Feeling: Empathy guides their decisions. They're like compassionate organizers, always considering others' needs.

Judging: Consuls love structure and tradition. They're reliable and dependable.

Key Traits:

Natural Caretakers: Consuls take care of everyone. They're like nurturing parents, ensuring everyone's well-being.

Duty-Driven: They fulfil responsibilities diligently. Consuls keep things running smoothly behind the scenes.

Harmony-Seekers: Consuls value harmony and cooperation. They're the glue that holds families and communities together.

Loyal Friends: They're reliable and loyal. Consuls are the ones you can count on during tough times.

In a Nutshell:

Imagine a warm host organizing a family gathering with love and attention to detail. That's the Consul—caring, practical, and always there for others. Consuls excel in nurturing relationships, creating stability, and making sure everyone feels welcome. If you meet one, appreciate their genuine kindness.

Virtuoso (ISTP)

Introverted: Virtuosos recharge by spending time alone. They're like independent explorers who value hands-on experiences.

Sensing: They focus on practical details. Virtuosos see the world through their senses—touch, taste, and smell.

Thinking: Logic guides their decisions. Emotions take a back seat—like skilled mechanics fixing a car.

Perceiving: Virtuosos embrace spontaneity. They adapt to the present moment.

Key Traits:

Practical Tinkerers: Virtuoso's love taking things apart and figuring out how they work. They're like curious inventors in a garage.

Adventurous Spirits: They seek thrills and new experiences. Virtuosos are the ones climbing mountains or fixing engines.

Resourceful Problem-Solvers: Virtuosos find creative solutions. They're the MacGyvers of real life.

Independent Mavericks: They march to their own beat. Virtuosos don't follow the crowd; they forge their own path.

In a Nutshell:

Imagine a skilled mechanic repairing a motorcycle engine with precision. That's the Virtuoso—practical, adventurous, and always ready to explore the unknown. Virtuosos excel in hands-on tasks, problem-solving, and living life on their terms. If you meet one, appreciate their resourcefulness

Adventurer (ISFP)

Introverted: Adventurers recharge by spending time alone. They're like creative artists who find inspiration in solitude.

Sensing: They focus on sensory experiences. Adventurers appreciate beauty, textures, and flavours.

Feeling: Emotions guide their decisions. They're like passionate poets expressing their inner world.

Perceiving: Adventurers embrace spontaneity. They go with the flow and follow their heart.

Key Traits:

Free Spirits: Adventurers dance to their own rhythm. They're like wildflowers swaying in the breeze.

Artistic Souls: They express themselves through art, music, or writing. Adventurers are the dreamers with paintbrushes.

Nature Lovers: Adventurers find solace in forests, beaches, and starry nights. They're the ones collecting seashells and stargazing.

Empathetic Explorers: They understand emotions deeply. Adventurers connect with others through shared experiences.

In a Nutshell:

Imagine a painter lost in a colourful canvas, creating magic with every stroke. That's the Adventurer—creative, sensitive, and ready for life's adventures. Adventurers excel in artistic expression, empathy, and savouring life's little moments. If you meet one, appreciate their unique perspective!

Entrepreneur (ESTP)

Extroverted: Entrepreneurs thrive in social settings. They're like energetic extroverts who gain energy from interacting with others.

Sensing: They focus on practical details. Entrepreneurs see the world through their senses—touch, taste, and action.

Thinking: Logic guides their decisions. Emotions take a back seat—like savvy businesspeople making strategic moves.

Perceiving: Entrepreneurs embrace spontaneity. They adapt quickly to changing circumstances.

Key Traits:

Risk-Takers: Entrepreneur's dive into new ventures fearlessly. They're like gamblers at the business table. **Action-Oriented**: They learn by doing. Entrepreneurs prefer hands-on experience over theory.

Resourceful Innovators: Entrepreneurs spot opportunities and turn them into profitable ventures. They're the visionaries behind start-ups.

Charm and Charisma: They're persuasive and magnetic. Entrepreneurs can sell ice to an Eskimo.

In a Nutshell:

Imagine a dynamic CEO launching a start-up, juggling ideas, and closing deals. That's the Entrepreneur—bold, adaptable, and ready to conquer the business world. Entrepreneurs excel in risk-taking, innovation, and turning dreams into reality. If you meet one, admire their entrepreneurial spirit!

Entertainer (ESFP)

Extroverted: Entertainers thrive in social settings. They're like lively extroverts who light up a room.

Sensing: They focus on sensory experiences. Entertainers appreciate the here and now—the taste of food, the beat of music, and the touch of a friend's hand.

Feeling: Emotions guide their decisions. They're like passionate actors, expressing their feelings openly.

Perceiving: Entertainers embrace spontaneity. They go with the flow and create fun wherever they are.

Key Traits:

Life of the Party: Entertainers bring energy to gatherings. They're like DJs at a dance floor, making everyone groove.

Creative Performers: They express themselves through art, music, or dance. Entertainers are the ones belting out karaoke or doing impromptu stand-up comedy.

Charm and Charisma: Entertainers captivate others. They're magnetic and draw people into their world.

Adventurous Spirits: They seek thrills and new experiences. Entertainers are the ones trying exotic foods or dancing under the stars.

In a Nutshell:

Imagine a bubbly actor stealing the show on stage, laughing, and making everyone feel alive. That's the Entertainer—vibrant, expressive, and ready to celebrate life. Entertainers excel in creating joy, connecting with others, and living in the moment. If you meet one, join the party!

So, we talked about 16 personalities in that we cover everything in relative to that specific personality all of us having one of the personalities out of that 16 personality but majorly we show only one, two or highest three personality but- but what if you had a superpower that you can use all 16 personalities and make your life better than ever okay so we made it practical in my opinion that superpower would be "SWITCH PERSONALITY". All of us contain all 16 personalities but all of us are able to use some of them but why? because we don't live in that moment to unrelease the personalities but how you release that power?? Do you know travellers are very good in their overall mind-health, emotional health and physical health "**THE MORE YOU TRAVEL THE MORE YOU INCREASE YOUR INTELLIGENCY AND THE MORE YOU USE YOUR PERSONALITY'S**".

Traveling can be a powerful catalyst for both brain development and personality growth. Here's how:

For the Brain:

- **Neuroplasticity**: When you travel, you're often faced with new challenges and unfamiliar situations that require problem-solving and adaptability. This can stimulate neuroplasticity, which is the brain's ability to form new neural connections throughout life.
- **Mental Resilience**: Overcoming the obstacles and uncertainties of travel can build mental resilience, enhancing your ability to cope with future stressors.
- **Cognitive Stimulation**: Learning about different cultures, languages, and environments can serve as a form of cognitive training, keeping the brain active and engaged.

For Personality:

- **Openness to Experience**: Travel exposes you to diverse ways of life, potentially making you more open-minded and willing to embrace new experiences.
- **Conscientiousness**: Planning and managing travel details can improve your organizational skills and self-discipline.
- **Emotional Stability**: By stepping out of your comfort zone, you learn to handle emotions in various scenarios, which can lead to greater emotional stability.
- **Extraversion**: Interacting with new people can enhance your social skills and make you more outgoing.

- **Agreeableness**: Encountering different perspectives and customs can foster empathy and understanding, traits associated with agreeableness.

In essence, traveling can enrich your brain function and shape your personality in profound ways, leading to a more fulfilling and well-rounded life.

Also opens the doors of the mind which were closed through years. So, do travel. I hope you all understand it

Does Love is a Scam?

Diverse Personality

This chapter is dedicated to you

My dearest busy street

PART – 6

Does Love is a Scam??

When we talk about "love," we're diving into a world of feelings, memories, and dreams. For me, if I had to sum up love in just one word, "ETERNAL" feels just right. It's like love that lasts forever, never fading away, no matter what life throws at us.

Think of love as a powerful force that doesn't care about time or distance. It's not just a quick feeling or something that comes and goes. It's like a hug that lasts forever, always there to hold us tight.

In the big story of life, true love isn't just a short chapter. It's like a never-ending book, with each page telling a new part of the story. This is what I mean by eternal love—it's a connection that never dies, like a song that keeps playing in our hearts.

But why "eternal"? Because real love doesn't stop. It keeps going, no matter what. It's like a light that never goes out, shining bright even when things get tough.

In a world where everything moves so fast, it's easy to forget about real love. We're surrounded by quick relationships and flashy gestures, but true love is different. It's not about big shows or fancy words. It's about the little things, like holding hands or sharing a laugh.

And remember, finding real love takes time. It's not something you can rush. You have to be patient and wait for the right moment. In a world where everyone wants everything right now, real love is a rare gem.

So, let's forget about the fast-paced world for a moment and think about what real love really means. It's not about flashy gestures or quick thrills. It's about the simple things, like being there for each other and never giving up.

In today's world, where everything moves so quickly, it's easy to forget about real love. But if we take a moment to slow down and really think about it, we'll see that real love is all around us, just waiting to be found.

- ➢ What is the real meaning of love?
- ➢ The power in the love.
- ➢ The story of bean and busy street.
- ➢ Why love is sometimes a scam??

Ah, love—the feeling that wraps us in warmth and makes our hearts skip a beat. It's like falling for a cactus; despite its prickly exterior, you're drawn to its beauty and forget about the thorns. Love has its ups and downs, but when you're truly in it, those challenges become just part of the adventure.

In a world where love seems tangled in a web of confusion, it's easy to forget its true essence. It's not just about fleeting moments of pleasure; it's about creating something lasting, something that leaves a mark on the world. True love has the power to shape history—to weave its way into the fabric of our lives and etch its story into the annals of time.

Love isn't just a feeling; it's a force of nature, capable of sparking revolutions and changing the course of human destiny. It's the driving force behind our greatest achievements and the deepest connections we forge.

But what's the science behind this magical phenomenon? Hold on tight, because we're about to dive into the electrifying world of love—the kind that makes your heart race and your head spin.

Love isn't limited to romantic relationships; it extends to our bonds with the world around us, from our furry friends to the objects that hold special meaning. When you truly love something or someone, your connection becomes a thread in the tapestry of history—a story woven into the fabric of time.

So, let's embrace the magic of love—the force that fuels our passions, inspires our dreams, and brings meaning to our lives. It's a journey filled with twists and turns, highs and lows, but through it all, love remains the heartbeat of our existence.

In our everyday lives, love motivates us to go the extra mile, to forgive, and to connect deeply with others. It's what pushes us to strive for better, to overcome challenges, and to cherish the people around us. Love is the quiet strength behind every major achievement and every significant relationship, making our journeys richer and more meaningful. It's not just an emotion; it's a driving force that influences our decisions, actions, and ultimately, our destinies.

Love is not always between girl and boy it could be towards a thing a non-living thing a pet but when you truly love somebody there were your names written in the pages in history

"Love creates history"

Picture this: Your heart, that squishy organ, suddenly decides to breakdance. It's like a tiny DJ spinning beats—boom, boom, boom. Love flips the switch, and suddenly, you're not just pumping blood; you're pumping feelings. It's like your chest is hosting a rave party, and your ribs are the bouncers.

But wait, what's behind this heart-thumping phenomenon? Science, my friend! It's all about the brain chemicals doing the tango. When you see someone attractive, your brain releases a cocktail of monoamines—dopamine, norepinephrine, and serotonin. These little troublemakers turn your heart into a disco ball, flashing neon lights and making it jitterbug like nobody's business

Now, let's talk brains. Love turns your Gray matter into a cosmic soda can. Pop! Fizz! Suddenly, you're thinking about someone 24/7.

Your neurons are doing the tango, creating mental fireworks. You forget where you put your keys, but you remember their favourite ice cream flavour. Priorities, right?

And guess what? Dopamine is the headliner here. It's the superstar responsible for pleasure and reward. When you're in love, your brain showers you with dopamine, like confetti at a rock concert. It's like your brain's way of saying, "Hey, you! Yes, you! You're doing great, keep loving!"

Ah, communication—the lifeblood of love. Texting becomes an Olympic sport. You analyse every "lol" and "ha-ha" like a cryptographer decoding ancient scrolls. "Did they mean 'I love you' or 'I'm out of milk'?" It's a dance—two thumbs waltzing across screens, hearts doing the Macarena.

And guess what? Norepinephrine and serotonin join the party. Norepinephrine amps up your alertness, like a double espresso shot. You're wide-eyed, ready to decode emojis and decipher hidden meanings. Meanwhile, serotonin—the mood stabilizer—keeps you from going full-on crazy. It's like your brain's way of saying, "Chill, dude, It's Just a text!"

Butterflies invade your stomach. Seriously, it's like a butterfly flash mob in there. They jitterbug, jitterbug, and suddenly, you're nervous around them. You trip over words, spill coffee, and forget your own name. It's adorable chaos—the kind that makes you feel alive.

And guess what? Serotonin is the choreographer here. It's the one responsible for mood regulation and appetite. But when you're in love, it goes haywire. It's like serotonin is doing the cha-cha with your gut, making it flip-flop and jitterbug. No wonder you feel like you're floating on air

Love has its soundtrack. You hear their name, and boom! Your brain cues up the playlist. Ed Sheeran croons, Adele belts out ballads, and suddenly, you're living in a rom-com montage. Every song becomes "your song." Even the microwave beeping sounds romantic.

And guess what? Oxytocin—the cuddle hormone—takes centre stage. It's the reason you want to snuggle, hold hands, and build blanket forts. Oxytocin whispers, "Hey, lovebirds, get close!" It's like your brain's way of saying, "Let's make memories, one cheesy song at a time!"

You build a blanket fort together. Yes, like kids. You huddle under fairy lights, sharing secrets. It's your safe space—a conspiracy against adulthood. Bills? Nah. Taxes? Nope. Inside the fort, it's all giggles, whispered dreams, and stolen kisses. The outside world can wait.

And guess what? Vasopressin—the commitment hormone—joins the party. It's like the fort's architect, making sure the walls are sturdy. Vasopressin nudges you toward loyalty and pair bonding. It's like your brain's way of saying, "Hey, you two, stick together!"

Love isn't algebra, but it's got its own equation: **You + Me = Infinity.** It's not about finding someone to complete you;

Now you all understand what is the real meaning of love and science behind it know we delve in the power of love have you heard the story of Dashrath Manji who breaks whole mountain for his wife when you understand how many powers does real love hold then you will understand how love can create history rather you waste your time on one night stand. today's generation is hyper filled lust inside the teenagers there were a thousand of barrel which are filled with lust today's generation prefer to have just a flint they just want to do time pass they really don't know what love is if you love a person but he/she not loves you but it's ok don't leave to love them if you really love a person love them for eternity true love has no breakup

If you had then I never meant to be true love.

Now I'll tell you the story one of my favourite story the story of 'bean and busy street'.

Okay the story revolves around a boy named "bean" and a girl named "Busy Street" that was their nicknames that they make for each other. the story starts when bean starts for the first time in the classroom when he saw girl then the whole story starts.

Bean had always been enchanted by her, the girl who occupied his thoughts day and night. He tried hard to muster the courage to talk to her, but each attempt ended in regret and missed opportunity. As half a season passed, bean decided to reach out to her online because he not enough courage to talk face to face. The girl that bean liked was majorly busy so, bean kept her name "busy street". How kooky it sounds!!lol!

Days turned into weeks, and the friendship between bean and the busy street flourished. They shared secrets, dreams, and countless conversations, deepening their bond. As the season drew to a close, bean found himself still unable to confess his true feelings. With the start of a new season, he resolved that this time he would not let fear hold him back. He had noticed the way she looked at him in the classroom, the lingering eye contact that made his heart race. bean believed that she felt the same way.

bean's love for her grew, blossoming into something true and profound.

Finally, the day came when bean decided that he would tell her his feelings online, lacking the courage to do it face to face. He began with a casual conversation, and after some time, with his heart pounding, he sent the message: "Hey busy street I had something to tell you, the reply came from busy street "yes go ahead" she didn't know what was coming up then without any message bean typed "I love you very much." His hands trembled as he hit send, and his heart raced, waiting for her response. Before she could react, she sent a message, but it wasn't about love. She tried to steer the conversation elsewhere, and bean, feeling disheartened, followed her lead. The 2 year of friendship ends in just 2 minutes

Despite his efforts, their distance increases. Bean apologized, hoping to mend their friendship, but she explained that she was overwhelmed and busy. Gathering all his courage, bean asked if she shared her feelings. The silence that followed was deafening. When he pressed further, she gently but firmly told him that she did not feel the same way. A last message that bean send to busy street that "you always take care and be happy always stay happy .Bean didn't cry he believed in his destiny that sure destiny would meet them again and if not, bean is always love with her

A whole day passed in silence, each minute a painful reminder of his unrequited love. Bean apologized again instead of distance bean, trying to salvage what was left of their friendship, but the damage was done. Their conversations dwindled and eventually stopped. Yet, bean's love for her remained unwavering. He made a promise to himself that he would never stop loving her, no matter the distance or silence between them.

Years went by, and bean's love only grew stronger. He vowed that if fate ever brought them back together, he would take her hand and bring her into his life forever. He dreamed of a future where they would marry and build a life together, filled with the love and happiness he had always envisioned. He promised himself that he would be there for her, always, never giving up on the love that had taken root so deeply in his heart.

Does Love is a Scam??

Bean's love story was one of enduring faith and relentless hope. And so, he counted the days—one by one, like beads on a rosary. Destiny might lead them back to each other, or it might not. But Bean's love remained—an unwritten chapter waiting for its happy ending. waiting for the right moment to bloom once more Though their paths had diverged, he never wavered in his promise. His heart beat for her, with a love that time and distance could not diminish. And so, **the real love that bean made for her he waited, holding onto the belief that someday, their story would have the happy ending he had always dreamed of. If not, then this story ended in the letters of the bean that he made for her busy street. he convinced himself that if she is not mine in this life surely, he could get her in another life with this sentence he convinced himself and build a very big dam of patience and faith in his "BUSY STREET".**

one of the poetries that bean wrote for busy street in his letter.

"In the moonlit night, my heart whispers your name,
But your love, like a distant star, remains untamed.
In the depths of my soul, a longing so deep,
For a love that's unrequited, a promise I can't keep.

Your smile, like the morning sun, bright and warm,
But in your eyes, I see a love that's torn.
I'm just a shadow in the moon's soft glow,
Yearning for a love that I'll never know.

Every beat of my heart sings your praise,
But in your world, I'm lost in a maze.
One-sided love, a bittersweet refrain,
A melody of longing, a never-ending pain.

In the silence of the night, I whisper my plea,
Hoping against hope, that you'll someday see.
But in this one-sided dance, I'll always be,
Lost in the echoes of a love meant to set me free."

May their paths intersect again, and may love find its way back to them—a love that defied seasons, silence, and the passage of years.

One-sided love can be an arduous journey, filled with hope, longing, and often, heartbreak. It requires immense courage to confess one's feelings, and even more to continue loving without reciprocity. This story teaches us that love is not just about being loved in return, but about the depth of one's own feelings and the strength to hold onto them, even in the face of adversity.

One-sided love is a powerful emotion, often unrequited and sometimes misunderstood. It is the kind of love where one-person harbours deep affection and admiration for another, without expecting anything in return. This love is selfless, patient, and enduring. It brings out the best in a person, pushing them to become more courageous, more expressive, and more resilient.

However, one-sided love also carries with it a profound sense of vulnerability. The fear of rejection and the pain of unreciprocated feelings can be overwhelming. Yet, those who experience one-sided love learn the true essence of love itself—it is not always about possession, but about cherishing the other person's happiness, even from afar.

One side love is the also example of doing true love where you want nothing from your partner expect some time and love [which contains care, respect, understandings and precious time]

The story of busy street and bean teaches us that love is not always you find easily sometimes you have to wait for it and kept patience for it no one knows for how much time.

Also, one major thing I saw in teens even in my own friends they never loved a girl/boy they just doing time pass and 10 in one if they were doing real love but if the partner left him, they became fucking sigma, alpha and another kind of shit they talked things like if she is not mine then I will not let her be someone else's. What a fucking crazy thing isn't? and also one thing more in this generation the kids doing love under 10-year boy were talking about his breakup with his friend how insane it sounds like this was the reality of this generation I know there were no age of doing love but if when the love is true now you are wondering at first, we can't even make a difference between love and the affection/crush I will clear this confusion Certainly! Let's delve into the intricate differences between **love**, **crush**, and **affection**, along with practical ways to identify which emotion you're experiencing.

1. Crush: The Spark of Infatuation

Characteristics of a Crush:

1. **Idealization**: You see the person through rose-tinted glasses, emphasizing their positive qualities while overlooking flaws.
2. **Physical Attraction**: Crushes often begin with a captivating appearance, a charming smile, or a specific trait that catches your eye.
3. **Intensity**: The initial attraction feels intense, like a sudden spark. Your heart races, and you daydream about shared moments.

4. **Short-Lived**: Crushes can ignite suddenly but tend to fade over time.

How to Identify a Crush:
- **Butterflies**: If being around them gives you nervous excitement (those fluttery feelings in your stomach), it's likely a crush.
- **Fantasies**: You imagine scenarios where you're together, even if you haven't had meaningful interactions yet.
- **Surface-Level Connection**: Conversations may be light and centred around getting to know each other superficially.

2. Affection: The Gentle Current

Characteristics of Affection:
1. **Comfort**: Affection feels like a cosy blanket on a chilly day. It's about feeling safe, cherished, and at ease.
2. **Familiarity**: Affection grows over time. It's the bond between old friends, family members, or even pets.
3. **Acts of Kindness**: Affection manifests through small gestures—holding hands, hugging, or cooking a favourite meal.
4. **Stability**: Unlike a crush, affection endures beyond fleeting moments.

How to Identify Affection:
- **Shared Memories**: You have a history together—a collection of shared experiences and inside jokes.
- **Consistency**: Affection doesn't waver; it's there during both highs and lows.

- **Feeling at Home**: Their presence feels comforting, like returning to a familiar place.

3. Love: The Symphony of Souls

Characteristics of Love:

1. **Emotional Depth**: Love encompasses joy, sorrow, passion, and vulnerability. It's a kaleidoscope of feelings.
2. **Acceptance**: Love embraces imperfections. You see the cracks in each other and choose to stay.
3. **Shared Dreams**: Love involves planning a future together—whether it's building a home, raising children, or growing old side by side.
4. **Selflessness**: Loving someone means caring about their well-being, even if it means sacrificing your own desires.

How to Identify Love:

- **Emotional Intimacy**: You share your deepest thoughts, fears, and dreams without hesitation.
- **Commitment**: Love isn't just about feelings; it's about choosing each other every day.
- **Seeing Beyond Surface**: You appreciate their flaws and quirks, knowing they're part of the beautiful whole.

Remember, self-awareness is key. Reflect on your emotions, observe how you feel when you're with the person, and pay attention to the quality of your interactions. Whether it's a crush, affection, or love, each holds its own magic. In summary, a **crush** is like a fleeting comet, **affection** is the steady glow of a candle, and **love** is the constellations that guide us through life. Each has its place, and recognizing them helps us navigate the beautiful chaos of human emotion. Now we are going to talk why sometimes love becomes a form scam or really love is a scam or not:

As I said before true love never be a included in a shit things and very purest form of true power that can push the limit the power of the person for just one person not like "nibba-nibbi" true love not asks a daily talk, daily meet it only demands purity and eternity.

"SO, LOVE IS NOT A SCAM"

Conclusion:

So, is love a scam? Absolutely not. True love is a rare and powerful force that goes beyond fleeting attractions and temporary infatuations. It's about patience, commitment, and a deep connection that lasts through the highs and lows of life.

In today's world, where casual relationships and superficial connections are often celebrated, understanding the real meaning of love is more important than ever. Love isn't just about grand gestures or physical attraction. It's the quiet moments of holding hands, the shared dreams, and the unwavering support through thick and thin. True love is eternal; it doesn't fade away but grows stronger with time.

Remember the story of Bean and Busy Street? It showed us that love is about cherishing someone even when they don't feel the same way. It's about holding onto hope and believing in the possibility of a happy ending. This kind of love requires immense courage and patience, but it also brings out the best in us.

To understand love better, it's essential to distinguish it from a crush or mere affection. A crush is an intense, short-lived attraction, often based on idealization. Affection is a gentle, comforting feeling that grows over time. Love, on the other hand, is a deep, emotional connection that accepts imperfections and dreams of a shared future.

True love isn't about constant communication or daily meetings. It's about the purity of your feelings and the eternity of your commitment. So, next time you wonder if love is real or just a scam, remember that genuine love creates history, changes lives, and stands the test of time.

In a world full of fleeting romances and temporary pleasures, strive for the kind of love that lasts forever. It's worth the wait and the effort because true love, once found, is the most beautiful thing you can ever experience.

PART – 7

People's 'hit

> *"I can be good as angel bad as evil but I can be both as in form of people"*~~Umang Jain
> *"Hell is empty and all devils are here"*—William Shakespeare

Welcome to the raw, unfiltered world of "Peopleshit". This isn't a chapter for the faint-hearted. It's a hard-hitting, no-holds-barred exploration of the real, often ugly, side of humanity.

In "Peopleshit", we're ripping off the band-aid and exposing the wounds. We're talking about the dirty deeds, the hidden secrets, and the not-so-pretty aspects of being human. We're putting the spotlight on our flaws, not to shame, but to understand and learn.

> *"We all are living the coal society that is dark filled with hatred one single flint of jealousy will burn you dare to be the diamond"*

This chapter is about the truth, the whole truth, and nothing but the truth. It's about accepting that we're all flawed, and that's okay. It's about understanding that it's these very flaws that make us human.

So, brace yourself. This is going to be a wild ride. But remember, it's only by facing the truth, no matter how uncomfortable, that we can hope to grow and improve. And in end of this chapter, you are able to decide people are shit or hit although it is neither accurate nor respectful to refer people as "SHIT" cause not every people are shit but not every people are hit though:

We are going to cover the role of things in human life to are capable to make people a piece of shit:

: proud thyself.
: love.
: lust.
: friends are a real shit.
: the universe of shit [social media]

: comfortable zone = hell.

: dream vs target.

: caged bird xx =caged human ✓

The Ego's Dance: Pride, Mortality, and the Spiritual Quest

In the bustling marketplace of existence, where souls barter emotions like precious gems, there stands a curious stall—the **Ego Emporium**. Here, egoistic wares are displayed—**pride, arrogance**, and the elusive **fear of mortality**. Let us wander these cobblestone streets and explore the harsh reality that stains our souls.

1. The Pride Merchant: A Velvet Cloak of Self-Worth

Picture Mr. Pride, the vendor. He dons a velvet cloak stitched with gold—a regal attire that whispers, "Look at me!" His stall boasts trophies, certificates, and accolades—a dazzling display of self-worth. The applause after a solo performance echo through our veins. But beware! Pride can morph into ego—the inflated balloon that blocks our view. It shouts, "I'm better than you!" We become the centre of our own universe, forgetting that galaxies swirl beyond our grasp.

2. The Ego Weaver: Illusions and Distorted Mirrors

Ego weaves a tapestry of illusions. It's the mirror that reflects only our best angles—the flattering filter on life's camera. "I am invincible," says Ego. It's the fortress we build to protect our fragile hearts. But within its walls, we're prisoners—afraid to peek beyond. Ego whispers, "You're separate from others." It's the illusion of islands in an interconnected sea.

3. The Fear Peddler: One Coin, Countless Nightmares

Now, let's visit the Fear Cart. Its wheels creak with uncertainty. The sign reads, "Fear of Death: One Coin, Countless Nightmares." Fear of death—the ultimate paradox. We fear the unknown, the cosmic curtain that falls on our life's play. It's the final act—the encore we can't rehearse. Why? Because we're wired for survival. Our lizard brains scream, "Stay alive!" But in this survival dance, we trip over our own feet.

"if you are able to see a vision to see yourself higher than today then also kept a vision to see yourself lower than today and most people forgot the second ones and after makes it an cursed stone which after ate all their success so think both side of the success" ~~Umang Jain

4. The Spiritual Alchemist: Acceptance and Humility

Amidst this market chaos, a hooded figure beckons—the Spiritual Alchemist. The potion offered blends humility and acceptance. "Embrace your mortality," says the Alchemist. "You're part of a cosmic symphony. When one note fades, others rise." Spirituality unravels fear's knots. It whispers, "Your stardust and fleeting moments. Death isn't an enemy; it's a companion." We're flawed, but we're also stardust pilgrims.

So, dear seeker of truth, confront the harshness, but also seek the light. For within our shadows lie constellations waiting to be discovered.

In the dimly lit corridors of existence, where shadows stretch and whispers echo, lies the raw underbelly of humanity. Brace yourself, for we're about to descend into the abyss—the unvarnished truth that stains our souls.

1. The Fragile Veil of Civilization

We strut upon the world stage, adorned in suits and silks, our smartphones clutched like talismans. But beneath this veneer, we're **savages**—hairless apes with nuclear codes. Our cities hum with electricity, yet darkness thrives within. We build skyscrapers while bulldozing forests. Our concrete jungles echo with loneliness, and our hearts ache for connection.

2. The Sins of Progress

We wield progress like a double-edged sword. **Technology** binds us, yet isolates us. We're connected globally, yet disconnected from our neighbour's. Our factories belch smoke, choking the lungs of Earth. We plunder her veins—oil, minerals, and innocence. Our progress leaves scars—deforested lands, poisoned rivers, and melting glaciers.

3. The Dance of Power and Greed

Behold the **tycoons**—modern-day pharaohs. They amass fortunes, their coffers overflowing. But their wealth is a black hole—it consumes light, leaving shadows in its wake. The poor huddle in slums, their dreams crushed like discarded wrappers. The gap widens—a chasm between penthouses and cardboard boxes.

4. The Masks We Wear

We don masks—the **smiling facade** at family gatherings, the stoic mask at funerals. Beneath, we're fractured—scarred by loss, haunted by regrets. Our social media feeds sparkle with filtered lives. But scroll deeper—the **anxiety**, the **depression**, the silent screams. We're drowning in likes, thirsting for love.

5. The Echoes of War

Wars rage—on battlefields and within souls. We're **armchair generals**, cheering from afar. But war isn't a game—it's blood-soaked soil, shattered homes, and orphaned children. Our history books are inked with conquests, but the pages reek of suffering. We're the architects of destruction, wielding missiles and ideologies.

6. The Clock Ticks Toward Extinction

Our planet gasps—a fevered breath. The **climate crisis** isn't fiction; it's our impending apocalypse. We're the arsonists, igniting forests, melting icebergs, and drowning coral reefs. The clock ticks toward extinction—of species, of cultures, of innocence. We're the witnesses—the jury and the condemned.

7. The Redemption Song

Amidst this bleak canvas, a note of hope—a redemption song. We're not just shadows; we're dawn's first light. Compassion stitches our wounds. Empathy bridges divides. Love—the cosmic quilt—wraps us in warmth. We're flawed, but we're also stardust pilgrims. Let's dance—between shadows and stars.

"If pride were a currency, would you bankrupt yourself or invest wisely?"

People think that love is bad thing they thought whoever love gets scammed but here a twist when you don't get scammed as I tell you in love is a scam? part do a genuine love if you do you never ever gets scammed here, I can tell you what happened in time pass love and what happened in true love

Alright, let's break it down with an interesting analogy. Imagine love as a journey on two different paths: the **Time pass Trail** and the **True Love Trek**.

Time pass Trail:

- It's like a casual stroll in the park. You're just there to enjoy the moment, not really going anywhere.
- You might pick up a few pebbles of experience, like learning what you don't want in a relationship, but that's about it.
- It's like eating fast food: quick, easy, but not very fulfilling in the long run.

True Love Trek:

- This is more like climbing a mountain. It's tough, challenging, but the view from the top is worth it.
- Along the way, you gain valuable knowledge like **patience**, **trust**, and **commitment**.
- You learn about yourself and grow as a person. It's like a nutritious meal that takes time to prepare but nourishes you deeply.

So, on the **True Love Trek**, you gain wisdom like:

1. **Self-Discovery**: You find out who you are when you're with someone who supports you.
2. **Teamwork**: You learn to work together, like two climbers tied to the same rope.
3. **Communication**: Just like hikers use signals, you learn to talk and listen effectively.
4. **Resilience**: You become stronger, able to weather storms together.

5. **Joy**: The happiness you find is like reaching a summit after a long climb.

In essence, time pass love might seem fun, but it's like a fleeting shadow. True love, on the other hand, is like a tree that grows slowly but gives fruits of knowledge and happiness for a lifetime.

All of us kept a very dangerous drug in their brain if it used once then it gets you to leave it and you all know it becomes a very dangerous thing to happening to your happening your brain and I call this drug "LUST" and if you are unable to control it. The lust is like a caged demon in your mind if once you open that cage the demon will take control over you and in this generation, the demon is common resultant crimes, rapes and strong discouragement let's understand what really lust is. Lust is a strong passion or longing, especially for sexual desires. It is often associated with intense or uncontrolled desires. These desires can be for anything such as power, money, objects, or most commonly, for another person. It's important to note that lust is not the same as love. Love is based on more than just physical attraction and involves feelings of affection and a desire for emotional closeness, while lust is primarily driven by desire and physical attraction. Please remember that it's normal and human to experience lust, but it's also important to be aware of its effects and manage it responsibly.

it controls you and that is the first step to get back to you worst life but how why lust can be detrimental to humans let's explore it:

1. **Distorted Priorities**:
    - Lust often clouds our judgment and distorts our priorities. It becomes an overpowering force, pushing other important aspects of life aside.

- Imagine someone neglecting their health, relationships, or responsibilities because they're consumed by lustful desires.

2. **Temporary Gratification**:
   - Lust provides instant gratification but lacks lasting fulfilment. It's like eating junk food—it satisfies the craving momentarily, but it doesn't nourish the soul.
   - People chase fleeting pleasures, sacrificing deeper connections and meaningful experiences.

3. **Selfishness and Objectification**:
   - Lust tends to objectify others. People become mere means to an end—a way to satisfy desire.
   - Relationships based on lust lack empathy and genuine care. It's all about "What can I get?" rather than "How can I give?"

4. **Emotional Turmoil**:
   - Lust can lead to emotional roller coasters. When desire isn't reciprocated or when the initial excitement fades, people experience disappointment, jealousy, and heartache.
   - It's like riding a wild wave that crashes eventually.

5. **Spiritual and Moral Impact**:
   - Many spiritual and ethical traditions caution against unchecked lust. It's seen as a distraction from higher purposes.
   - Lust can erode our inner peace and disconnect us from our true selves.

In summary, while desire is natural, unbridled lust can harm our well-being. It's essential to recognize its pitfalls and seek healthier, more balanced connections

Remember this, dear reader: Lust is a masquerade ball, and we're all masked dancers. But sometimes, beneath the glittering facade, we glimpse our own brokenness. And in that fractured reflection, we find the truth: Lust is a hunger that can devour us whole, leaving only echoes in its wake.

FRIENDS ARE A REAL SHIT!!!!

Friends when we hear this word it seems familiar to you, we all have one or two friends or "best friends" in which you rely most and also opens the secret that you don't want but it's okay they are your friends they are not going to tell your secrets to anyone isn't? now further I don't need to elaborate it you all know how in this era friendship is just a kinky word that is roaming without any purpose now - days friendship offers you pain, the fire of hatred and lots of anxiety and some other ingredients which is required in today's friendship so, don't gets trapped in a so called friendship it is like obsidian it can harm you but first you don't understand it and everything stays normal you feel no pain but after some time you suffer a lot of pain which is unable to bear .

"An insincere and evil friend is more to be feared than a wild beast; a wild beast may wound your body, but an evil friend will wound your mind." – Buddha

Don't think your life gets easy when you got a friend when you face every single problem by your own you became the best variant of yourself

THE UNIVERSE OF SHIT ----------- #SOCIALMEDIA

Social media is one of the vital reasons why we are unable to run our mind and lost our ability to focus and our reaction time is getting reduced day by day but as I said this generation is habitat to live in comfortable zone, they watch reel, shorts, chatting with a girl trying to impress people posting story frequently making streaks if streaks break, I think the world will going to end !!! lol! In this generation there is a lot of bullshit motherfuckers which are just drown in the world of social media they seriously giving the key to control them and one thing they are doing good for hackers they are giving their privacy without any cost later they regret and then ask why I should do it wish I hadn't post where I am going wish I hadn't made a house tour wish I hadn't made snaps of my private things wish I hadn't wasted my time in doing that shit I am you will regret one day

The world of social media, while seemingly bright and engaging, can sometimes cast a shadow that's often overlooked. Here's a simple explanation of some of the harsh realities:

1. Comparison Trap: social media often presents an idealized version of reality, leading to constant comparison with others. This can result in feelings of inadequacy and low self-esteem.

2. Privacy Concerns: Personal information shared on social media can be misused, leading to privacy issues. It's like living in a glass house where everyone can see into your life.

3. Cyberbullying: The anonymity of social media can sometimes give rise to cyberbullying, causing emotional distress.

4. Addiction: The constant need for validation through likes and comments can lead to an unhealthy addiction to social media, affecting mental health and productivity.

And most important the era of fakeness is also originated with the fucking social media and have you ever wondered that why in your social media vulgar content spreads most but why because you like it? and because they wanted to show you and then you capture shit in your mind when the shit goes overdoes you go and do masturbation for this us government filed a case against Mark Zuckerberg ongoing court case in the US has put the spotlight back on Mark Zuckerberg's Meta – the parent company of Facebook and Instagram – for allegedly failing to protect children from sexual predators on the social media platforms.

The case is ongoing in New Mexico, United States, concerning child abuse on Meta's Facebook and Instagram apps.

Though the case dates back to December 2023, Meta's rival X's billionaire owner Elon Musk flagged the issue recently by reshairing a post that showed a screenshot of a news item, 'Meta documents show 100,000 kids sexually harassed daily on Facebook, Instagram'.

The case filed with the First Judicial District Court of the County of Santa Fe by New Mexico's attorney general, Raul Torrez, against Meta as well as its founder Mark Zuckerberg calls the company's social media platforms a "breeding ground" for predators who target children for human trafficking.

It claims Meta platforms enable the distribution of sexual images, grooming, and solicitation. "Teens and preteens can easily register for unrestricted accounts because of a lack of age verification. When they do, Meta directs harmful and inappropriate material at them. It allows unconnected adults to have unfettered access to them, which those adults use for grooming and solicitation," it says.

Referring to unsealed legal filings, The Guardian reported in January Meta estimated about 100,000 children using Facebook and Instagram received online sexual harassment each day.

Zuckerberg's social media platforms have repeatedly faced criticism for weak oversight of the content that may impact youth mental health and threaten child safety.

A former employee of Facebook, Arturo Be jar, told a US Senate subcommittee in November 2023 that Meta's top executives, including Zuckerberg, ignored warnings for years about potential harm to teens on its platforms.

Separately, attorneys general from 33 US states filed a case against Meta in 2023, accusing the company of refusing to shut down the majority of accounts belonging to children under the age of 13 while collecting their personal information without their parents' consent.

The latest case accuses Meta of failing to curb the sexual exploitation of children on its platforms while targeting the "age-based vulnerabilities" of children by adopting algorithms that are addictive to young users.

"Meta's platforms are the social media equivalent of an addictive drug from which young users cannot break free. Meta knew that these design features fostered addiction, anxiety, depression, self-harm, and suicide among teens and preteens," it said.

A Meta spokesperson denied in a statement that its platforms put children's well-being at risk.

"We use sophisticated technology, hire child safety experts, report content to the National Centre for Missing and Exploited Children, and share information and tools with other companies and law enforcement, including state attorneys general, to help root out predators," said Nkechi Nnaji, adding that Meta removed hundreds of thousands of accounts, groups and devices for violating its child safety policies.

Remember, while social media can be a great tool for connection and information, it's important to use it responsibly and be aware of its potential downsides. It's always a good idea to take regular breaks, maintain privacy, and remember that what you see online may not always reflect reality.

if you have rich mindset, you generally don't go on a way to show off you live the moment without taking any fucking snaps nor post anything that's why there is a huge difference between you and super riches you give your privacy for free and they spend money to maintain their privacy how crazy it is!

Comfort Zone = Hell

Comfort zone is the zone where all people go and if they are unable to come then they come with their disturbed fate from that hell zone. **The comfort zone is a psychological state where individuals feel safe, familiar, and unchallenged.** While it provides a sense of security, it can also be a barrier to growth and success. Let's delve into why stepping out of the comfort zone is crucial for achieving success:

1. **Stagnation and Plateau:**
   - **Comfort, although pleasant in the short term, can often lead to complacency and stagnation.** When we remain within our comfort zones, we limit our potential for growth and progress.
   - People who stick to routines devoid of risk find their progress plateauing. Without challenge, there is no impetus to learn new skills or expand limits.

2. **Fear of Failure and Rejection:**
   - **The comfort zone shields us from anxiety and fear.** When faced with the possibility of failure or rejection, our primal survival program urges us to retreat.
   - **Anxiety is throbbing inside us,** making it hard to move forward and meet challenges. The internal voice continually shouts, don't! does anything click in your mind it also has same symptoms like in the self-doubt phase it is also a main reason why we dig a hole of self-doubt for ourself if we live in a comfort zone.
3. **True Capabilities Remain Hidden:**
   - **Stepping out of the comfort zone reveals our true capabilities.** Unless we bravely face challenges, we'll never know how far we can go.
   - Courage to withstand anxiety is essential. Only then can we seize opportunities and make the most of life's prospects.
4. **Success Requires Action and Resilience:**
   - **Success demands constant action, perseverance, and resilience.** Choosing the harder path—embracing challenges—leads to greater fulfilment.
   - By venturing beyond the familiar, we open-door to personal and professional growth.

In summary, breaking free from the comfort zone is essential for reaching our full potential. It involves facing fears, learning, and pushing beyond limits. So, dare to step out, embrace discomfort, and achieve the success you deserve!

Whether your life becomes "HELL"

Dream vs Target

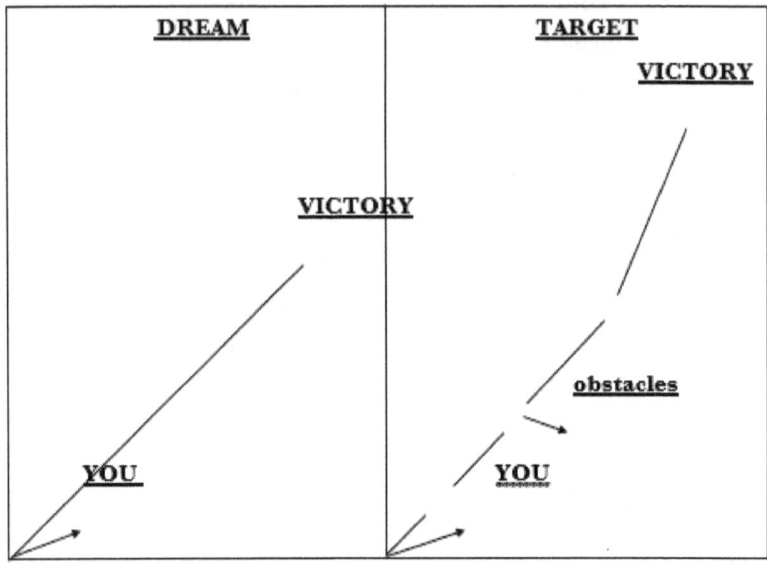

The hill of real life

Dream!! When we dream of something that is out of in your hand we wish to have it and sometimes we'll do work for that to accomplish it but after that it only stays fresh during your sleep you failed to do it you treated it like a dream that's why .Do you know that what is the power of our words and what impact occurs when we say anything your words are like coin of the vending machine [the brain success vending machine] when you put the coin of dream you get the success in dream but if you put the coin of target it gives you success in real life . dream seems easy to see and easy to accomplish but target is tough to do but it has many obstacles and the success is also big comparative to dreams as we saw in "The hill of real life"

Certainly! Let's boldly compare **dreams** and **targets**:

1. **Nature:**
   - **Dreams** are ethereal, intangible, and often surreal. They emerge from the depths of our subconscious during sleep, like whispers from the universe.
   - **Targets**, on the other hand, are concrete, purposeful, and firmly rooted in reality. They are the bullseyes we aim for with unwavering determination.
2. **Origin:**
   - **Dreams** arise spontaneously, unbidden. They weave intricate narratives, blending memories, desires, and fears.
   - **Targets** are deliberate choices. We set them based on aspirations, priorities, and strategic planning.
3. **Flight vs. Focus:**
   - **Dreams** allow us to soar beyond boundaries. We sprout wings, defy gravity, and explore uncharted realms.
   - **Targets** ground us. They demand discipline, focus, and calculated steps. No shortcuts allowed.
4. **Emotion vs. Strategy:**
   - **Dreams** evoke emotions—joy, fear, longing. They're the canvas of our heart's desires.
   - **Targets** require strategy. We map out routes, gather resources, and navigate obstacles.
5. **Outcome:**
   - **Dreams** may dissipate like morning mist or linger as inspiration. They're the seeds of creativity.

- o **Targets** yield results. They transform sweat into success, effort into achievement.
6. **Boldness:**
    - o **Dreams** whisper, "What if?" They beckon us to leap into the unknown.
    - o **Targets** declare, "I will." They propel us forward, step by deliberate step.

In summary, **dreams ignite our imagination, while targets ignite our determination.** Both are essential—dreams fuel our spirit, and targets guide our journey

Learn to control your words as I said words plays a vital role in shaping our mind from now don't say I had a dream to became a millionaire instead of that say I had an aim to be a millionaire that is called power of words.

Caged bird XX = Caged human ✓

Peoples are like to live in a cage that people made and we are all living in that cage that peoples made we have not our freedom we think only but in reality, we are overwhelmed with many cages that are not easy to escape we can also call this the era of caged humans we are in a cage of our mind, we are in a cage of others mind, we are in a cage of our fear and society. We are going to see the 3 cages

Psychological Caging

1. Mental Health Struggles

- Conditions such as depression, anxiety, and PTSD can feel like an invisible cage. Sufferers often find themselves trapped in a cycle of negative thoughts and emotions, struggling to break free from their mental confines.

2. Addiction

- Whether it's substance abuse or behavioural addictions like gambling, these dependencies act as powerful cages. Individuals often feel powerless to escape the grip of their addiction, which dominates their lives.

3. Digital Overload

- Our increasing reliance on technology, particularly social media, can lead to a sense of being 'caged' by screens. The pressure to stay connected and the constant influx of information can be overwhelming, affecting mental health and personal relationships.

Societal and Cultural Caging

1. Economic Inequality

- Economic disparity acts as a societal cage, limiting opportunities and mobility for those in lower income brackets. The struggle to break free from poverty is a persistent battle against systemic barriers.

2. Discrimination and Prejudice

- Racism, sexism, and other forms of discrimination create societal cages that restrict individuals' potential. These prejudices confine people to certain roles and opportunities based on their race, gender, or other characteristics.

3. Constricting Social Norms

- Traditional social norms can be stifling, dictating how individuals should behave, what careers they should pursue, and how they should live their lives. Breaking free from these expectations often requires immense courage and resilience.

Metaphorical Caging

1. Conformity and Compliance

- Societal pressure to conform can feel like a cage, stifling individuality and creativity. People often suppress their true selves to fit in, leading to a loss of identity and fulfilment.

2. Fear and Insecurity

- Personal fears—of failure, rejection, or the unknown—can be the most restrictive cages of all. These fears can prevent individuals from pursuing their dreams and realizing their full potential.

3. Workplace Environments

- Modern work culture, with its relentless pace and high demands, can create a sense of entrapment. Employees may feel stuck in jobs they dislike, driven by financial necessity or lack of better opportunities.

Breaking Free from the Cages

Understanding these various forms of caging is the first step toward liberation. Here's how we can begin to unlock these cages:

1. Policy and Legal Reforms

- Addressing physical caging through fair policies and legal reforms is crucial. This includes prison reform, combating human trafficking, and creating pathways out of poverty.

2. Mental Health Support

- Increasing access to mental health resources and reducing stigma can help individuals break free from psychological cages. Support systems and professional help are essential.

3. Digital Balance

- Encouraging a balanced approach to technology use can mitigate the effects of digital overload. Digital detoxes and promoting real-world interactions are vital.

4. Educational Initiatives

- Educating people about the impacts of discrimination and rigid social norms can promote inclusivity and acceptance, helping to dismantle societal cages.

5. Personal Development

- Fostering self-awareness and personal growth can empower individuals to overcome their internal fears and insecurities, breaking free from metaphorical cages.

By addressing these diverse aspects of caging, we can strive towards a future where individuals are free to live, express, and develop to their fullest potential, unbound by the invisible bars that currently hold so many captives.

Peoples are not a piece of crap or shit at first, they are good but after some time there is some things which make them a piece of shit as we discussed before but here is also a one important thing everything and for every situation of his life, he is responsible.

"Every person is responsible for their happiness as well as sadness"

Neither I will able to bring happiness nor I will able to bring sadness to you.

Now we are moving ahead to the very darkest shit works done by people's

1. THE SUPERIORS.

2. THE MONEY GOD.

3. THE EDUCATION SYSTEM XX ➔ THE SLAVE SYSTEM

CONCLUSION

THE SUPERIORS

As I mentioned in the first part about the superior's thing and I described you that we all are in a cage of those superiors but again that question stuck who are those fucking superiors?

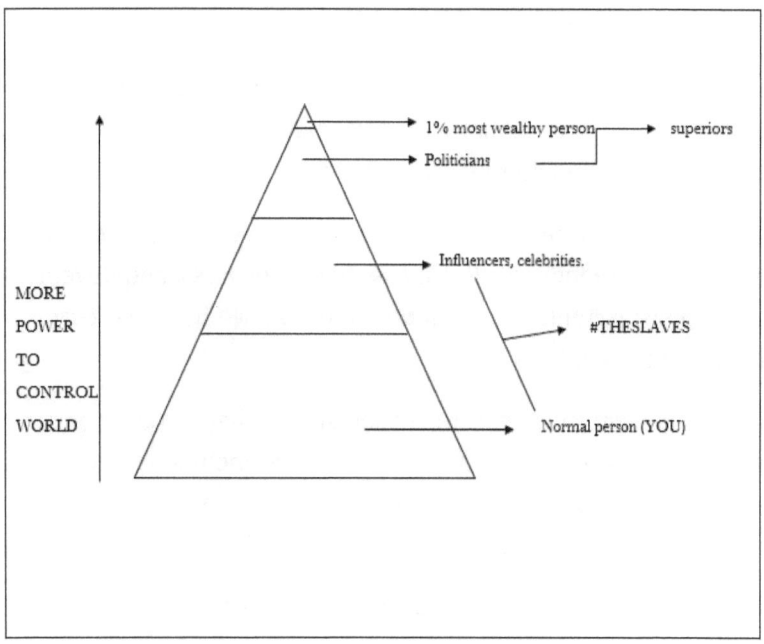

I call this figure "The dominant triangle" but why it has several reasons why I named this dominant triangle as I described this figure dominant triangle so our mind break it down and tells us a meaning that a triangle is dominating isn't the 1% is only a complete triangle and is able to dominate the whole space that is the basic reason of giving this name a dominant triangle now we'll understand some realties with the help of this "dominant triangle" as we are able to see that there is four levels each level is dedicated to its role and its quantity let's break it down:

The Dominant Triangle: Unmasking the Puppeteers

Alright, my fellow truth-seekers, let's peel back the layers of reality like an onion at a therapy session. You've got questions, and I've got conspiracy theories—let's dance.

Act 1: The 1%—The Illuminati's Afterparty: At the tippy-top of our pyramid lies the 1%. These folks are so rich they use hundred-dollar bills as napkins. They control more strings than a marionette puppeteer. Their secret handshake involves offshore bank accounts and a sprinkle of unicorn tears. And guess what? They're the only complete triangle in this circus. Why? Because they're the architects of the cage—the ones who build walls while sipping champagne. But here's the cosmic joke: there's no cage for them. Nope. They're like VIP guests at the Matrix afterparty, sipping virtual cocktails and laughing at our 9-to-5 struggles.

Act 2: The Politicians—Wizards with PowerPoint Presentations: Next up, the politicians—the middle managers of our cosmic corporation. They're like wizards with PowerPoint presentations, promising change while juggling campaign funds. Some are big shots—presidents, prime ministers, and senators. Others are local heroes—the mayors, council members, and dog-catcher-in-chiefs. But guess what? They're all part of the same pyramid scheme. They weave laws like spider silk, trapping us in their bureaucratic web. And when they're not busy filibustering, they're practicing their best "I care about the environment" speeches in front of a mirror.

Act 3: The Influencers and Celebrities—Pop Culture Pied Pipers: Now, let's shimmy down to the influencers and celebrities. They're the trendsetters—the ones who tell us what to wear, what to eat, and which cryptocurrency to invest in (spoiler: it's not Dogecoin). They're like modern-day oracles, except instead of cryptic prophecies, they drop skincare routines and avocado toast recipes. And we listen. Oh, we listen. Because nothing says "I'm woke" like buying the same organic bamboo toothbrush as Gwyneth Paltrow.

Act 4: The Rest of Us—Hamsters on the Wheel: And finally, the largest chunk of our cosmic pie—the normal folks. We're the hamsters on the wheel, the worker bees, the ones who pay taxes, mortgages, and gym memberships we never use. We live in the cage—the one we don't even question. Why? Because it's cosy. It's familiar. It smells like microwave popcorn and existential dread. We're like goldfish in a bowl, swimming in circles, occasionally bumping our heads against the glass, wondering if there's more to life than Excel spreadsheets and cat videos.

The Bold Conclusion: So, my fellow cage dwellers, let's raise our invisible glasses to the 1%, the politicians, the influencers, and even the Kardashians (because why not?). Maybe, just maybe, we can break free from this cosmic choreography. Maybe we can pirouette out of the pyramid, moonwalk into the unknown, and find a new dance floor—one where the music isn't on repeat, and the DJ takes requests. Until then, keep questioning, keep dreaming, and remember: life's too short to be a puppet.

The money God:

Money a very essential piece of paper that have power to make or ruin your whole life but how many is more dominated than human although people are the ones who create that piece of paper but further it becomes more dominating more powerful than people but why??

In today's century peoples are so much obsessed with money but there is also a fact this generation is too lazy but they want to achieve something big with these fairy-demands are only be done with a money

Money, oh money—how you've become the modern deity for so many! It's a tale as old as time, yet as fresh as the daily news Oh, money, money, money. It's like that friend who promises to make life a party but sometimes ends up spiking the punch. Why do we treat it like it's the boss of us? Well, let's break it down in plain talk, shall we?

Money: The Bossy Bestie Imagine money as that pal who's always got the coolest gadgets and throws the best parties. You want to hang with them because, they make things happen. But then, you start thinking, "Do I need this friend to have a good time?" That's where it gets tricky. We start believing that without money, life's a dud. And that's how money becomes the big cheese, the head honcho, then... you get the picture.

The Dark Side of the Dough Now, here's where the plot thickens. Moneys lIke a magic wand—it can get you a castle, a shiny carriage, maybe even a royal title. But what happens when the magic goes poof? Suddenly, you're left holding a stick, and the castle's just a pile of cards. That's the dark side of dough. It can vanish, and when it does, it can take your peace of mind with it.

Deadly Dollars? So, how does money turn from lifesaver to life-taker? Picture this: you're so busy chasing bills that you forget to live. You miss out on laughs with friends, sunsets, and the simple joy of a good cup of tea. And for what? A few extra zeroes in the bank? Here's a thought: can you take it with you? Last time I checked, those pockets in your funeral suit aren't that deep.

Keeping It Chill with the Cash Alright, let's not get all gloomy. Money's not the villain in our story—it's just playing its part. It's all about how you direct the play. Use it to spread some love, help a buddy out, or fund that dream project. Just remember, it's a tool, not the trophy.

So, why do we make money our god? Maybe because we forgot how to worship the little things. And isn't it funny how we call it 'making a living' when sometimes it feels like it's doing the exact opposite? Food for thought, eh?

Keep it real, keep it balanced, and don't let those greenbacks turn you green with envy. After all, the best things in life—like this little chat we're having—are free. a little more to chew on in the banquet of life. Just remember, when it comes to money, it's not about the size of your wallet, but the wealth of your heart.

Money: The Great Illusionist Money's like that magician who pulls rabbits out of hats and coins from behind your ear. But sometimes, it feels like the real trick is how it disappears when the bills come out to play. It's like, "Abracadabra! Now you're broke."

The Street-Smart Take on Cash Here's some street-smart wisdom: Money can buy a house, but not a home; it can buy a clock, but not time; it can buy you a position, but not respect; it can buy you a bed, but not sleep; it can buy you a book, but not knowledge; it can buy you medicine, but not health; it can buy you blood, but not life; it can buy you sex, but not love. So, you see, money isn't everything, and it often causes pain and suffering. I tell you all this because I am your friend, and as your friend, I want to take away your pain and suffering... So, send me all your money and I will suffer for you. A truer friend you will not find.LOL!!!

The Hustle and Bustle for Bucks In the hustle for that cash, we're all running a marathon with no finish line. It's like, "Run faster, earn more, and maybe you'll be happy." But isn't it ironic how we're sprinting so hard we miss the scenery?

The Sarcasm in the Savings And let's chuckle at the irony of savings accounts. We're stashing away money for a rainy day, but what if it never rains? Are we just collecting water for a storm that's never coming?

If money is the root of all evil, why do they ask for it in church? It's a question that makes you go hmmm, doesn't it?

The Real Riches So, let's wrap this up with a bow of wisdom. Remember, the real riches are the ones that don't crinkle or fold. They're the hearty laughs, the shared stories, and the warm hugs. They're the moments that stick to your soul, not your wallet.

And there you have it, a dollop of wisdom mixed into our money musings. Keep it light, keep it wise, and remember, the best investment you can make is in the currency of kindness.

But after all these discussions you are not going to agree that money is not your god society makes pressurize to all of us that money is too much important, I do agree on this but I do not agree money is a god. in today's era everything money can buy the self-respect to whole human thanks to our fucking society for making money our god. For because of this mentality, we all doing this fucking rat race a never-ending rat race if you tried to escape you were criticizing you were seen failure in the eyes of society there were no value thanks to our "SUPERIORS" AND THEIR FOLLOWER'S

Today's generation is fully covered with all kind of shit that can exist one of them are usually known as "the great rat-race" no-no that is not a game of rats that is a game of humans how fucking peoples are they doesn't even left rat for my point of view it should not be the great rat race it should be the great slave race. people are overwhelmed with work and if he/she was a child society is making mould I which they learn to be slave if you think you are not slave so take one page write your whole day routine every day for at least 1 week see that routine is going or not now some of you are saying in study we need discipline so we need the same routine and same time management isn't okay let's move it forward now you got 95% I n higher studies now you are in college you also gets passed with impressive grades now the time of your job we assume you find a job now the routine is still going as same as when you are a kid now as an adult nothing changes but the place where you serve your slavery. I do agree money fulfils all your needs but if you keep in your mind that "money gives honey" then I guess you are no more distracted to things

You can buy everything with money I mean everything that exists in this world for that don't fall in a trap of money make a trap to make money fall in your trap once Robert Kiyosaki said "don't work for money make money to work for you". But how for that you need to do things which gives you monthly income like you rented your home, opens a grocery store and hire a manager basically make multiple income sources as much you can if that goes well then it you can finally taste honey.

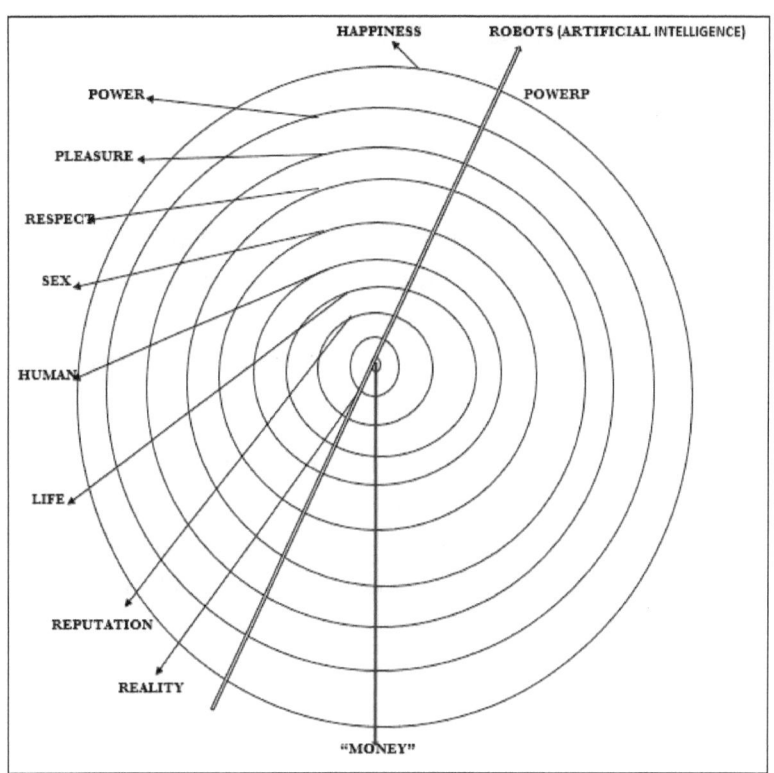

THE MONEY SYSTEM

The money system is the best figure to depicts how powerful money becomes. the deeper you go the more you know who says money can't buy happiness cause in today's generation nobody thinks it for everyone it is a paradise so I stated happiness on the first disc we can bring or take happiness with help of money expect you are a monk. The second circle I stated power cause you all know power = money or money = power the more money you have the more power you get. The third disc I stated pleasure who disagrees this fact that money does not give pleasure. the 4th disc respect some people think respect has to earn over years but I don't agree because you see politicians, they just throw a bunch of money in the public the public started to lick their ass. On the 5th disc I stated sex I think you all know I do not need to elaborate it. the 6th disc humans. peoples are always hungry of money for money they can anything they are able to be servant so the 6th disc is given to humans. On the 7th disc I stated life because as I said humans can take life for money and can give life for money [bankruptcy].8th disc reputation is used to be the one of the precious gemstones in the olden times but todays it was just a pet of money. On the 9th and last disc, I stated reality money has a power to create or change the reality that is why I stated it on 9th disc.

And the point describes the money which has enough power to revolve around his ass but you are also able to see the intersection I draw which is of ai what does that mean?? Any guesses?? Okay so I stated ai because they are just beyond this, they had no happiness no reality no sex no reputation no life and I think in future this money system could be the one of the prominent reasons of the dominance of ai in human if the society never solve the problem and never decrease the negative intensity of money maybe the future could we worst then we'll ever thought.

"Money is a great servant but a bad master." – Francis Bacon

The slave education system

The Slave Education System: A Critical Look

The education system, once a beacon of enlightenment, has become a conveyor belt that churns out compliant individuals. It's time to break free from this cycle and reimagine education. Let's explore the flaws of the current system, compare it to ancient Gurukul education, and discuss how we can empower students to think beyond societal norms. Our modern education system, often criticized as a "slave education system," seems designed to mould students into perfect workers for the future, rather than fostering independent thinkers and innovators. This system, which has remained largely unchanged for decades, imitates and confines the minds of students. When someone dares to question it, society often shuts them down, maintaining the status quo.

The Contrast with Ancient Gurukul System

In ancient times, the Gurukul education system in India was vastly different and arguably superior. Gurukuls focused on holistic development, teaching a wide array of skills—everything from academics to physical training, ethics, and self-reliance. Students lived with their teachers and learned through hands-on experiences, storytelling, and deep discussions. This system encouraged critical thinking and personal growth. Our education system clings to outdated practices. Despite technological advancements, the core remains unchanged. Ancient Gurukuls, on the other hand, emphasized holistic learning. Students imbibed not only knowledge but also life skills, ethics, and values. We must blend the best of both worlds.

The Stagnation of Modern Education

Fast forward to today, and our education system seems to have stagnated. Despite technological advancements and societal changes, the core of education remains focused on rote learning, standardized tests, and conformity. Students are taught to memorize information rather than understand it, to follow instructions rather than think independently. This approach prepares them to fit into predefined roles in the workforce, effectively making them modern-day slaves to the economic machine. Traditional education moulds students into obedient workers. It stifles creativity, discourages questioning, and perpetuates a culture of compliance. Imagine a world where students are encouraged to explore, question, and innovate—where their minds are free to roam beyond textbooks.

A System Resistant to Change

Why hasn't this system evolved? Partly because it serves powerful interests. An educated, critically thinking populace is harder to control. It's easier to manage a society where individuals are trained to follow orders without question. When students or parents challenge this system, they often face resistance or outright dismissal, reinforcing the cycle of compliance and conformity. Students learned practical skills—farming, carpentry, music, and philosophy. Today, we focus on academic excellence, often neglecting essential life skills. Let's reintroduce vocational training, financial literacy, and emotional intelligence into our curriculum.

The Shift in Student Priorities

Adding to this, today's students are often distracted by societal pressures to conform to superficial standards. Social media glorifies aesthetic appeal and relationships, overshadowing the importance of intellectual and personal development. This shift in priorities further supports the notion that the current education system is not geared towards true learning and growth, but rather towards maintaining a certain social and economic order. Education sometimes prioritizes aesthetics over substance. Students chase popularity, fashion, and relationships.

The Need for Change

The need for a shift in our education system is clear. We should draw inspiration from the Gurukul system and modernize it to fit today's context. Imagine an education system where students are encouraged to ask questions, think critically, and develop a wide range of skills. A system where learning is a lifelong process, not just a means to a job.

Beyond Exams

Exams shouldn't be the sole measure of success. Gurukuls evaluated students holistically—through discussions, projects, and real-world applications. Let's move away from rote memorization and embrace experiential learning.

Questions to Reflect On

- Why do we continue to follow an outdated education model that doesn't serve our needs?
- What can we learn from ancient education systems that focused on holistic development?

- How can we shift societal values to prioritize true education over superficial achievements?

For me the more percent you got in this education system the more you are capable of being slave. If you get me in a wrong way, I am saying in a wrong way buddy. For me this education system is a fucking piece of shit!!!!!

Conclusion

In conclusion, the current education system acts more like a factory producing obedient workers rather than nurturing creative, independent thinkers. It's time we recognize this and strive for an educational paradigm that values curiosity, critical thinking, and personal growth over mere conformity. Only then can we break free from the chains of the "slave education system" and foster a society of truly educated individuals. Breaking free from the chains of the education system requires collective effort. As students, parents, and educators, we can create a new paradigm—one that values curiosity, critical thinking, and holistic growth. Let's liberate minds, nurture hearts, and build a brighter future.

In my point of view the higher your percentage the higher you have chances to be slave but that does not mean education is a bad thing but the way it comes it is bad I only prefer how much knowledge a person carry not how much percentage. Although there were a kind of toppers who knows everything in academics but not a single knowledge of world do you ever wondered why mostly backbenchers hit not toppers, I observed it very precisely toppers like to lick teacher's ass but not backbenchers they does not follow cage of the school helps them to expand their mind if you are studying with this education system it's better to quit it rather your mindset develops like a servant.

The slave education system

This is the last page and I know this book is also a another kind of book for you doesn't matter how much books you read when you don't apply it in yourself believe me there is not even a single book can really help you see you are born in this life fulfilled with pain , suffering and happiness you are a stranger for every new sun and you just let go the thing people set their goals but never accomplish it but why cause people set their goals higher sorry- sorry highest you tell me you are a broke right and you are setting goals that you want to became a millionaire then you are working on it but to be honest in the next 7 decades you never be instead of that you try I want to be millionaire so I had to break down it and then accomplish the checkpoint goals it better helps you . you can't run 10 km without saving your breath you make the checkpoints then stop there then move forward.

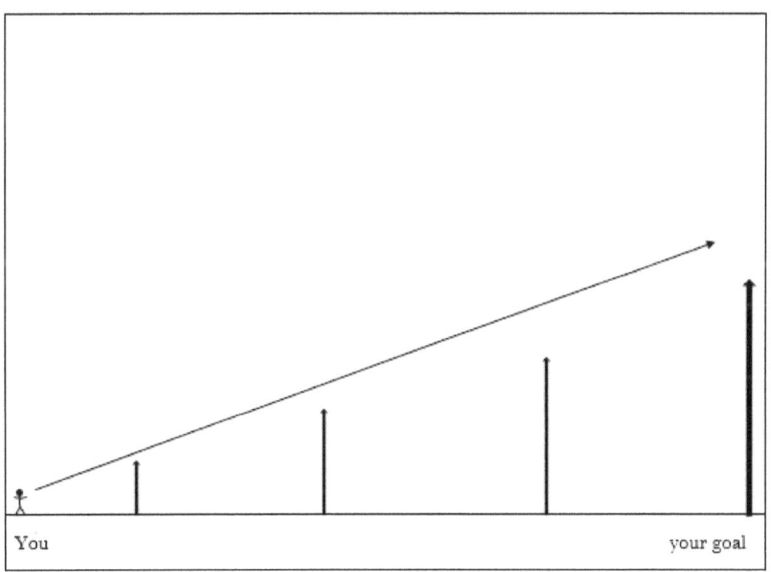

The checkpoint success

With every check point you are getting closure to your real success and the results are getting good. When you break your goals in smaller ones then your brain help to achieve them if you thought that you have to became the world strongest person so firstly your mind says "fuck you I am not going to do it. it is bigger than your status" but if you thought I have to build body if I became consistent then I'll became strongest person then you are just giving your mind a same question but from a maze that brain doesn't want to complete no matter how big or small your goal is break it on a very low level and then try to achieve them smaller ones it keeps you in a safer zone.

The slave education system

After all of the conclusion of the chapters and passing the chapters, we came to know that

PEOPLE ARE SHIT

The end……………. see the next page I had a paradox for you.

Hope you like this book but before going I had a paradox for you

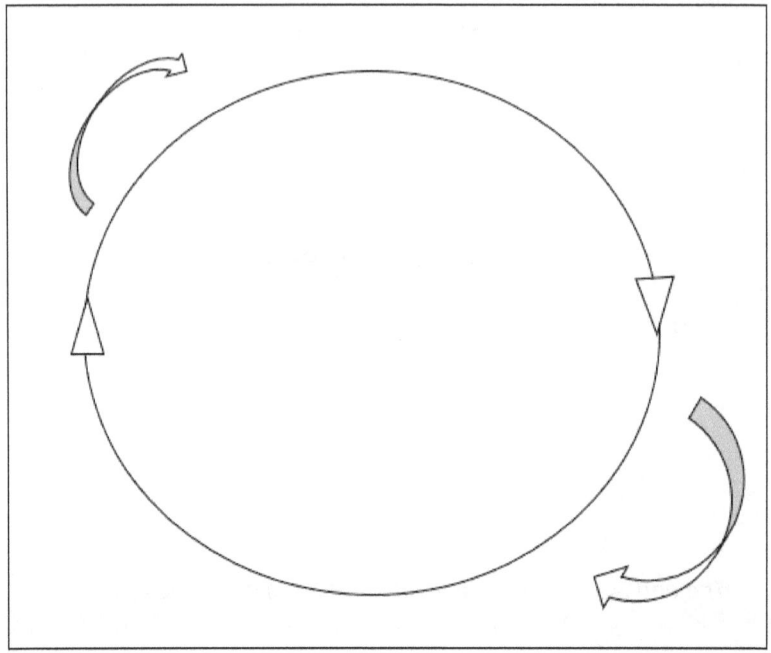

I call this circle paradox so tell me there are 2 persons walking on a circle on a same distance so can you tell me who is walking behind and who is walking forward to that person?? Think about it If you are unable to think I can tell you but not in this book I am writing the new book named: JUST IMAGINE it is fully mind bended sci- fi book make sure you'll solve this until my book came.

www.ingramcontent.com/pod-product-compliance
Lightning Source LLC
LaVergne TN
LVHW041949070526
838199LV00051BA/2953